# NABOKOV
# A Bibliography

BOOKS BY ANDREW FIELD
Pages from Tarusa, editor
Nabokov: His Life in Art
Fractions
The Complection of Russian
Literature, compiler
Nabokov—A Bibliography
Nabokov: His Life in Part
(forthcoming)

# NABOKOV
## A Bibliography

ANDREW FIELD

McGraw-Hill Book Company

New York    St. Louis    San Francisco

Düsseldorf    London    Mexico

Sydney    Toronto

123456789BPBP79876543

**Library of Congress Cataloging in Publication Data**
Field, Andrew, 1938–
    Nabokov—A Bibliography

    1. Nabokov, Vladimir Vladimirovich, 1899–
—Bibliography.
Z8608.6.F53      016.813'5'4      72-10473
ISBN 0-07-020680-5

210635

# Table of Contents

The first comprehensive Nabokov bibliography was compiled by Nabokov's German translator, Dieter E. Zimmer, and published by the Rowohlt Verlag, Nabokov's German publisher, as a "Christmas and New Year's present" for friends of the author and of his publisher in December, 1963. This pioneer effort was followed by a revised and enlarged edition in 1964, and it is this little volume, with its soft, warm blood-adust cover on which is printed the solitary signature of its subject, which has remained until now the only orthodox comprehensive bibliography of Nabokov's works. Vladimir Nabokov—Bibliographie des Gesamtwerks, impressive enough in itself, is all the more admirable for the fact that Mr. Zimmer has no Russian, and yet, with a bare Cyrillic alphabet and the information given him by Mrs. Nabokov, he tracked through thousands of pages of The Rudder, the Berlin émigré newspaper of which Nabokov's father was a founder and where more than a decade of early V. Sirin poems, stories, plays, and articles appeared.

It was the omission of and the need for more detailed listings—Mr. Zimmer, searching for Sirin in a nimeity of over-brown old newspapers in an unfamiliar tongue in the Bavarian State Library and with many books and journals unavailable or unknown to him, can in no way be faulted for these lacunae—that led me to append a new bibliography to my 1967 book, Nabokov—His Life in Art. The intent of that bibliography, however, is quite different from the aims of the Zimmer bibliography and the one in hand; it seeks merely to demonstrate in the shortest possible space the enormous range of Nabokov's writing, without any translations. This early descriptive bibliography of mine still has value for those who wish a precise but readable picture of what Nabokov has written.

Nabokov—A Bibliography would seem, on the other hand, to defy sustained reading. It contains all the additions of my former bibliography plus several score new entries found in Nabokov's trunks of personal papers that had, until this year, been in storage in Ithaca, New York. Full transliterations are given as well as prior appearances of works in journals, subsequent reprintings, and translations.

It would seem to defy sustained reading, and yet, safely out of its maze, perhaps one of the most complex and extensive bibliographies of any major twentieth-century author, I can recommend certain recondite charms of this impersonal work. (Thomas Frognall Dibdin wrote a "bibliographical romance" in 1809, and a few authors have played with this spartan genre with some success; not only Nabokov, but many writers from the time of Homer have loved lists and have felt their obscure incantatory powers more clearly than the scholars.) If the English first lines of the early Russian poems have a pleasantly familiar sirenic lilt, this is because Nabokov could not resist the temptation to render these first lines in metered poetic form himself. May a bibliography cite itself?

It is fascinating to follow the spread of translation by country, date, and quantity. *Lo li t'ai*, in Chinese, *light of my I*. The anthropologically inclined may lift an eyebrow at the weedlike profusion of Arabic translations, all unauthorized, of *Lo*. My favorite discovery is the way in which one Russian novel of Nabokov's, *Otchayanie*, was translated into the English *Despair*, from which a French translation under the altered title *La méprise* was made, and in turn a Spanish translation *El engaño* (the telltale mistake!) was grafted from it. Thereby a Russian émigré novel, by an author more concerned than most with problems of translation, traces the zig-zag path of translations of translations of translations by which so many books made their way into Russian in previous centuries.

Owing to the tricks of history and language, Nabokov's work waited many years for a bibliography—by contrast, Edmund Wilson, only four years Nabokov's elder, received a full bibliography twenty-six years ago—and if Nabokov bibliographies seem to come now breathlessly upon each other I can see no special harm in this. The world and Nabokov's reputation can suffer a few more works such as The Critical Response to the Work of V. Nabokov in South America (submitted in partial fulfilment of . . .).

Nabokov—A Bibliography has been divided into fourteen sections. These are: Collected Poetry; Poems—Separate Appearances; Novels and Short Story Collections; Short Stories—Separate Appearances and Translations; Plays and Scenarios; Memoirs; Essays, Book Reviews, and Criticism; Lepidoptera; Chess Problems; Miscellaneous Collected Reprintings; Translations; Letters and Interviews; Epigrams and Casual Items; and, finally, there is a first attempt at a bibliography of reviews of Nabokov in the émigré press and also a brief guide to émigré publications. The transliteration system used is a modification of the Library of Congress method, and an English-Cyrillic comparison chart has been included.

The Gold Coast, Australia                          Andrew Field
May 5, 1972

# A Bibliographer's Casebook

Until now the 1963–64 bibliography by Dieter E. Zimmer (Reinbek. Rowohlt) has been the only systematic bibliography of Nabokov's work, although a simplified bibliography which I appended to my 1967 book, Nabokov—His Life in Art (Little, Brown; Hodder & Stoughton), contained more than eighty items which were not in the Zimmer bibliography and, together with corrections and fuller entries, over three hundred additional listings. (Cursory bibliographies have also appeared in the French journal L'Arc [No. 24, Aix-en-Provence], Nabokov—The Man and His Work [University of Wisconsin Press, 1967], and Nabokov's Congeries [Viking, 1968] but they are of no significance.)

The historical advance in precision in this bibliography can, therefore, easily be measured by comparison of it with the Zimmer bibliography and my own 1967 effort. I am in a very real sense grateful for this perspective, without which even bibliographers and scholars of Russian literature might not be able to realize what has been involved in these searches for needles in hayfields where too often there has not even been the luxury of a haystack. There is a danger that such a casebook may produce the impression either of boastfulness or, more often, of defensiveness. Neither effect is intended. Rather, I would like simply to catalogue as carefully as possible all the problems and the particular lacunae that are to be found in this work in the hope that by so doing I may aid a future bibliographer.

The obvious problem presented by a bibliography of Vladimir Nabokov is that no one, or two, or even ten libraries contain the scattered publications of the Russian emigration between 1919 and 1940. A vital early publication such as Russkoe Èkho, in which the young Nabokov's work appeared, has only been located in a partial holding in Czechoslovakia. Many numbers of Berlin publications such as Russkoe Èkho and Nash Vek may well have perished during World War II: and a newspaper such as Segodnya, published in Latvia, now exists only in the partial holdings in Helsinki and at the British Museum. In any event, the location of a publication such as Segodnya in a Latvian library today presents the bibliographer with certain political problems; and this same consideration renders the location of a 1918 poem (K svobode) which Nabokov recalls having published "in some Yalta newspaper," difficult enough in any case, quite impossible under the present political circumstances.

Apart from utilization of the existing bibliographies and other bibliographical aids (chief among them the Index Translationum published yearly by The United Nations), three main avenues of research were followed in the preparation of this bibliography. There was the consultation of Vladimir Nabokov's own notebooks and certain papers and correspondence, where many clippings and references to poems and stories were found which would otherwise surely have been lost for all time; there was search work done in the main and obtainable émigré newspapers and publications (this largely in London, Boston, and New York); and lastly, there were many inquiries made of publishers' permissions departments and foreign rights departments to obtain information about excerpts, reprints, and translations, and also inquiries to the national libraries and principal university libraries of many countries around the world to obtain information about editions which had evaded previous recording. It has not been possible, of course, to detail the method of verification for each item, but every effort has been made to double- and even triple-check sources wherever possible, and, whenever questions remain, a full account of the available data and circumstances is given. Because Russian émigré journals are not familiar even to many Russian scholars, a full glossary on this subject has been appended; for information as to where these rare journals may be obtained the reader is referred to L. Foster's Bibliography of Russian Émigré Literature. There is no possibility of listing the scores of libraries and publishers who provided help, but I would like to thank them all collectively and especial thanks should be given to the librarians and staff of the University of Queensland, the National Library of Australia, the University of Chicago, Harvard University, the New York Public Library, Helsinki University Library, and the British Museum.

The system of cross-references which has been employed always leads back to an item's first appearance in print. (This is particularly important for tracing down those items which have undergone a change in title.) Details of reprintings and translations follow the entry of each item's first appearance. The cross-references also help to order the web of multi-purpose titles (such as *Spring in Fialta*, which is a short story, a Russian collection, and the title of collections of short stories in two other languages which are not congruent with the Russian volume). Care should be taken not to confuse internal reference numbers, which occur in the center of the page, with the cross-reference numbers. Whereas the cross-reference numbers lead back to the original appearance, reference to the total number of appearances may be found in the index. Works of the same title but different classification are differentiated by type face, e.g., the original appearance of a novel or a collection is always shown in bold Roman type.

The order of categories reflects, first, the natural chronology of Nabokov's writing career and, second, the comparative importance of the secondary groupings. Certain exigencies helped to create a reasonable semblance of simplicity—for example, translations of short stories are listed under separate appearances because to do otherwise would have been to sacrifice any sense of the original collections. Other practical decisions included strict rules of grouping by which, for instance, a book such as Nabokov's Congeries cannot have a place in Novels and Short Story Collections because it is a collection of reprinted works rather than a direct translation from Russian to English or an original work. In such cases, however—and there are many—a cross-reference note is provided in a place where a work might otherwise be expected to be found.

A basic decision was to structure the bibliography so that, with the important exceptions of English and Russian editions, which appear first in the list of translations, the bibliography arranges works by country of publication rather than by language. This usage (while following that of the Zimmer bibliography) differs from the generally accepted practice of arranging translations by language. But it was my intention in planning this work to have the finished bibliography be more than a guide to the full *oeuvre* of Nabokov. For example, there has come into existence in recent years an interesting "sociology of literature" which, in the hands of scholars such as Robert Escarpit in France, is making attempts to chart and analyze the origins of fame and the movement and duration of reputation in literature. This bibliography should certainly offer opportunities to such sociologists, and hopefully the material will be more workable in their hands for being located more precisely in a geographical sense. Finally and most obviously, as this bibliography has gathered materials from libraries around the world, so it will eventually find its way into many of these libraries as a reference work, and, because of its attention to Nabokov's appearance in journals of specific countries, many readers—in South America, to give but one instance—will find a much broader availability of his writings than they otherwise may have expected. And as an important corollary of this fact, it will now be possible to do more specific investigations of the literary influence of Nabokov as well as of the critical reaction of various cultures to his works.

As I began work on this bibliography, I was put in the position of going over steps which I had already taken. As I prepared my critical study of Nabokov in 1965 and 1966, I at first intended a purely critical study with full scholarly background but unencumbered by any scholarly apparatus. This intention was basically realized; yet, as I became progressively more and more aware of the lacunae in the Zimmer bibliography, I bowed before the need to append my own bibliography. In that bibliography it was wholly sufficient to list, for example, *Three Chess Sonnets*, as the poems in fact appeared under that heading in The Rudder. But for a complete bibliography it was necessary to go back and locate the first lines of those three poems, and in general to make more precise scores of such references which I first put forward in 1967. One benefit of this annoying necessity to retrace my steps, of course, was that in doing so I was able along the way to double-check many items, remove certain errors, and even find a few things which had evaded my first investigation. One loss was that certain sources which I had used were for reasons of time, location, and space no longer as freely available for consultation.

One of the most challenging and rewarding areas of research was the period between 1916 and 1926, that is, Nabokov's first appearances in print. Particularly valued was the discovery of an excerpt from **Mashen'ka** which was published before the novel. Of more substantive value and excitement were the discoveries of a second early poem in English and—through perusal of the British Museum's index to periodicals published in Berlin during this period (though later this item was listed, without first lines, in the Foster bibliography of Russian émigré literature)—of the literary almanac Vereteno in which no less than four heretofore entirely unknown Sirin poems appeared. For the strict bibliographer, however, this discovery brought its own problem: the author now recalls that at least one, perhaps more, of these poems appeared earlier in some journal or newspaper (Russkoe Ėkho?) which has not come to memory or to light. Occasional items, such as two poems which were printed in brochures for the benefit of charities, would have been totally lost were it not for their chance inclusion among the author's saved papers, many of which, however, were lost during World War II. Such happy if almost totally obscure discoveries will of course be of no further bibliographic "use" to anyone until such time as there is a full collected edition of Nabokov's work.

Memory (Nabokov's) and chance have had particularly to be relied upon in regard to early appearances. Thus, Nabokov's recollection of "poems in the Messenger of Europe and Russian Thought 1915–16," as recorded in the Zimmer bibliography in 1963, puzzled me and caused me to state in my 1967 book that "a most careful check of these numbers, however, has failed to reveal any Nabokov poems for these years," but a fortuitous discovery uncovered a poem in Russian Thought for March–April 1917. As it was always valuable to be forced by previous lacunae (some of them due to my own carelessness) to retrace my pre-1967 steps, so, too, it proved wise to allow a chronological amplitude in my searches. Sometimes a minor translation reference had to be abandoned owing to the enormous amount of time and money which would be required to solve the problem—for example, the short story *Terra incognita* was said in another bibliography to have appeared in the Bolivian journal Arco, Volume 8, No. 48, April 1964; but it develops that No. 48 appeared in September 1964, and Volume 8 pertains to 1966. Sometimes, when a matter of absolute bibliographic importance was involved, it was necessary to follow the search through to a conclusion. One of the most formidable of these searches was for a single letter to the editor which appeared in the Cornell University student newspaper, the Cornell Sun, while Nabokov was a faculty member there. The letter happens to pertain to an academic dispute of some significance in Nabokov's biography, but Nabokov himself did not recall the year, and the other party to the dispute declined to help me. Thus literally hundreds of working hours were spent searching for a single letter to the editor written in October 1958. Not infrequently problems were caused through the appearances of works or translations in publications which were themselves supplements to other publications. Here, too, luck played a major part in whatever successes there were. When one letter of inquiry to the Danish journal Magasinet was by mistake delivered to the Magasin du Nord (a large department store), it came to light through the kind help and good memory of one of its employees that Magasinet was a now-defunct supplement to the newspaper Politiken. But the lack of good fortune such as this has so far blocked all attempts to locate the unauthorized Chinese translation of **Lolita** which appeared in Taiwan. Sometimes, where a book could not be obtained, chance all the same brought forth bits of necessary information from unexpected corners—a European edition which is evidently no longer available in European libraries came to light in a Greek library. Inquiries to several libraries in India, where no translations of Nabokov's work were known even to the author, yielded no less than three Indian-language editions. Numerous unanswered letters to Israel finally brought information about the Polish translation of **Lolita.**

The circumstances and exigencies of émigré publications caused many problems to the bibliographer. One very basic problem concerns the change from the Gregorian calendar effected by the Soviet government after 1917. This change, involving an addition of thirteen days, was belatedly accepted by the émigré press between 1921 and 1923. Many émigré newspapers, however, made a practice of printing both dates (for instance, December 16 [December 3]), the Old Style date usually following the new date in parentheses, and it is to be expected that these double dates are the source of some bibliographical confusion. Briefly, the composition dates given for works prior to 1921 are Old Style; and dates between 1921 and 1923 are (hopefully) all New Style, too. Caution should be exercized here inasmuch as not all entries for this period could be personally verified for date.

Another serious problem in regard to dates arises because journals such as Contemporary Annals and The Fire-Bird began by imitating the monthly issues of similar publications in pre-revolutionary Russia, but soon it turned out that this was an infeasible aspiration, with the result that a journal such as Contemporary Annals may begin with monthly notations but subsequently changes to a different system of enumeration.

Mention should also be made of an inconsistency in the manner of newspaper listings: simple dates are employed for Nabokov's appearances in The Rudder (here actual newspapers were consulted), but very often issue numbers had to be used for other papers, in particular The Latest News, where clippings and the issue numbers were all that was available. Still another good instance of a bibliographical problem is the journal Russian Thought which appeared in the early 1920s. Apart from the fact that there are two other émigré publications bearing this same title to which Nabokov contributed—the one being the pre-revolutionary journal, the other being the émigré newspaper in Paris which is still being published—there were four places of publication for different numbers of this journal (Sophia, Prague, Berlin, Paris); the months of the journal are printed in roman numerals on the title pages of each issue in such a way as to appear to be (as I mistakenly assumed in 1967) volume numbers; and finally, there is no pagination in one issue, and so the page reference had to be counted by hand. These pedantic concerns, as every practicing scholar and librarian will realize, are essential points of information if these obscure émigré works are to be obtained, where they may be obtained at all, with any reasonable ease.

A great deal might be said for the inclusion of all possible available information pertaining to all entries. But in regard to the important question of pagination, it was not a practical undertaking for a bibliography of this scope, because a very high percentage of the reprintings and translations were not available for actual inspection by the bibliographer. What has been done then is to list the page numbers of Russian and English editions (first appearances only), and also, wherever possible, the page numbers for uncollected works. For the sake of some minimal uniformity, too, the titles of series and special identifications for individual publishers (a practice particularly common in regard to paperbacks) could not be noted. Special comments have been included wherever I feel that the additional information is of bibliographic importance; also, for the reader who may not be familiar with Nabokov's work, such items as particularly long poems have been pointed out.

The transliteration system which has been employed (see chart) is a slight variation on the Library of Congress method, on the assumption that this is the system most readily comprehensible to the greatest number of English-speaking people. The system used by Mr. Nabokov himself in his two-volume Commentary to Eugene Onegin, having certain features of the Czech method of transliteration and certain individual features, has been respected as his own scholarly signature. His system appears only in the listings of collections of short stories where both the order of contents and the transliteration method used by him are adhered to strictly. On the other hand, it would have been catastrophic from a bibliographical point of view in a work such as this to have reproduced the old system of spelling which was still used for some but not all émigré journals, and so Contemporary Annals is rendered as Sovremennye Zapiski (this being the form now used in virtually all bibliographies and scholarly works) rather than Sovremennyya Zapiski.

Another point on which a necessary difference between the bibliographer and his subject had to be maintained was in regard to the author's fairly free renditions into English of his Russian titles. The early poem *Gerb*, later included in **Poems and Problems,** is elegantly rendered by Nabokov himself as *Blazon*, but it is important to register as well the more prosaic

*Coat of Arms.* The English version of the novel **Podvig** may have gained immensely through the interpretive translation of its title **Glory,** but it is also necessary for the bibliographer to record the more prosaic and literal translation, **The Exploit.** This record of more literal titles is particularly important wherever previous references have been made to the work in print. Nabokov himself has arranged the English translations of the first lines of all his Russian poems so that they metrically reproduce the Russian.

Through access in my researches to some notebooks and albums of Mr. Nabokov's and also those which were kept by his mother it was possible to ascertain the dates of composition of very many of the early poems. Each has been recorded at the point of a poem's first appearance with one important exception, namely, the poems in **The Empyrean Path,** for here it was discovered that most of the poems are in chronological order and so, by listing the dates at this point, it is possible to establish the probable date of composition for many of the undated poems. Unfortunately, because many of the Nabokov manuscripts were some years ago donated to the Library of Congress in the United States where they are removed from scholarly examination until fifty years after the death of the author, it was not possible to obtain composition dates for later poems and short stories in like manner. A very small number of contradictions of composition and publication dates has arisen between the materials I have gathered and the information supplied by Mr. Nabokov himself. It is puzzling, for example, that a manuscript copy of the short story *The Busy Man* which I examined is dated a bit later than the story's appearance in the Paris newspaper The Latest News. Where such matters have not been successfully resolved, it has been thought best to leave the contradiction with an indication of it. Apart from these dates, only a few other historically important dates (such as that of the last poem that Nabokov wrote before leaving Russia) have been included. There were many instances in which I had at my disposal not only the year but also the month of a book's publication, but it was decided, again on the grounds of uniformity, not to supply this information because it is lacking for so very many other entries. Only in such instances, already mentioned, where there is a possibility of confusion of dates and volumes because of inconsistency or unorthodox usage has the necessary additional information been supplied in parentheses.

The problems presented by translations and permissions could be chronicled at great length. A few items will suffice. There is a large gap in regard to information about reprints and permissions for the period beginning in 1936 when Nabokov works first began to be translated into English and ending in 1958–59 when Nabokov's publishers became G. P. Putnam's Sons in the United States and Weidenfeld & Nicolson in Great Britain and the Commonwealth. For this interim the publishers of such works as **The Real Life of Sebastian Knight** and **Bend Sinister,** New Directions and Henry Holt, have no records of permissions, though it is reasonable to suppose, as they do, that there may have been none, or at any rate few. Another of Mr. Nabokov's publishers, Doubleday, where many permissions have almost certainly been given (one of the Nabokov books which they published was **Pnin**), has kept no record of the early permissions. To all intents and purposes this admittedly minor portion of Nabokov's bibliography has been lost forever.

Foreign translations were among the most difficult items to track down. Library inquiries in regard to the known Czech translations of Nabokov's works in the 1930s met with no success, although one of these translations did turn up among the author's papers. A slightly different type of Czech bibliographic problem appears more recently, during the period of the Dubček government: numerous works were contracted for and some actually did appear, but for many there is some question as to whether or not they were printed. One interesting discovery was that two translations of the same short story appeared at a distance of several years in the same French journal. Prepublication extracts and permissions to reprint excerpts sometimes offered up from time to time "ghost" entries: a permission was requested and granted by Putnam's for an anthology entitled *Stories from the Sixties*—and *Stories from the Sixties* did appear, but in the meantime the Nabokov material had somehow disengaged itself from the project; and similarly, a permission to print a portion of **The Gift** in the *Hudson Review* was granted but never used. These instances which have been caught should serve as sufficient warning for the existence of other such errors.

After not a little difficulty, an important confusion about four early poems, two dedicated to Blok and two to Bunin, was resolved. The second Bunin poem had been noted by me in my 1966 research in The Rudder, but the author himself doubted the existence of such a second poem. Eventually it was found again, and it developed that the dedication was to Bunin, but the dedication does not serve as the actual title as it does in the other poem. In the case of the two Blok poems it was found that a single long poem had earlier been printed as two short poems, a practice that was followed on several other occasions as well. Dedications, which are of obvious biographical interest, have been included for all printed poems, but there are instances in which poems have been found with a dedication in manuscript that does not appear in print, and these dedications have not been included. There is only one dedication in Nabokov's Russian prose (of **The Gift,** to his mother), and all of Nabokov's books in English after **Lolita** have been dedicated to his wife.

Comparison of the three bibliographies will show that much essential information in the Zimmer and first Field bibliographies has been corrected or made more precise. While, because of its generic usage, it must remain in the drama section, **Agaspher** is now described not as a play but merely as a poetic prologue to a staged entertainment. As one of the dividends of the indexing of this bibliography—this had not been done with the previous two—it was possible to separate works with the same title (e.g. *Spring, Native Land* etc.), of which there are a surprising number. A further advance to greater precision is the reference to the circumstances of various editions. There have been four privately printed editions, and though two of these are editions of poetic juvenilia, two are Russian reprintings which, it must be assumed, are not for general sale. There have also been destroyed editions. One French edition published by Gallimard had to be withdrawn from sale because of a contractual misunderstanding with the American publisher New Directions. An imperfect English edition of one of Nabokov's books was withdrawn and destroyed. One of the most dependable sources of withdrawn and bowdlerized editions is Sweden. A survey of the Swedish entries will quickly reveal that Nabokov—whose name has been mentioned in connection with the Nobel Prize for Literature for many years— has been more poorly served there than in virtually any other of the highly literate countries in Europe, and one wonders to what degree this is consistent with Swedish treatment of other major writers. The language from which a translation has been derived is given wherever there has been indication of this fact on the title page. Not only have many Russian works been translated into various European languages from their English translation, but also another intermediary language can sometimes be detected. These factors, too, will presumably be important to the sociologist of literature studying the spread of the "influence" of Vladimir Nabokov.

The unauthorized translations present self-evident problems for the bibliographer, since very often (especially in the case of **Lolita**) these are editions for the marketplace and railway station which do not find their way into libraries. The publishing houses which issue such translations are almost always transitory, and, even where they are not, such publishers can hardly be expected to accede to requests for bibliographical data, the publicizing of which could bring them legal difficulties. Yet a certain amount of progress has been made in this regard.

It is generally true that works written in Russian prior to 1940 are signed with the *nom de plume* V. Sirin, and that works written in English after this date are signed Vladimir Nabokov. However, there are exceptions (early works signed V. V. Nabokov and Russian poems signed Vasili Shishkov and Vivian Calmbrood), and these divergent signatures have been noted.

There are certain problems in establishing the correct genre for a work. There are "short stories" (listed as such in the Zimmer bibliography) that are really excerpts from novels. Another widely printed "short story" is actually a chapter taken from Nabokov's autobiography **Speak, Memory.** In the early poetry collections there are several poems, e.g. *La Belle Dame sans Merci*, which are really translations. A minor problem is presented by Russian poems with titles in French or English, which may appear as incomplete entries to the rapid eye. There are instances where a work has an important sub-title such as "translation from Zoorlandian" or "Ein Spiel mit dem Schicksal," and these have been indicated. Numerous peculiarities of various publications—such as when a work has been printed in a holograph photo—have been noted. Russian titles have all been translated, and titles as well as first lines have been given in instances where there is a duplication or even a possible confusion. In addition translations of foreign titles are given in instances where they differ significantly from the original.

Perhaps the most important lacuna in the compilation of this bibliography has been the failure to trace down the original appearances of seven short stories which doubtless appeared in Russian émigré publications in France in the 1930s. The author remembers that these seven short stories appeared in The Latest News, and as full an examination of the files of this newspaper as would be desired has not yet been possible. It is always possible that the stories appeared in another newspaper, or that some of them did not appear at all prior to their appearance in book form. Fortunately, since all the stories are available, it is a matter of academic interest, and hopefully this problem too will be solved in time.

The first appendix to this work presents the only compilation ever attempted on Russian émigré reviews of Nabokov prior to 1940 (with the inclusion of some important post-1940 items). This is obviously a major scholarly need. What I have been able to accomplish must be regarded as merely the first bibliography of Russian reviews of Nabokov, that is, as a rough draft in preparation for a more comprehensive listing at some later time. An excellent bibliography of reviews of Nabokov in English prior to **Ada,** by Jackson R. Bryer and Thomas J. Bergin, Jr., is included in Nabokov—The Man and His Work (University of Wisconsin Press, Madison, Milwaukee, and London, 1967). Finally, a smaller aid is furnished by an appendix of descriptions of Russian newspapers and journals in which Nabokov's works have appeared.

In Nabokov—His Life in Art I wrote that the bibliography while "still not complete . . . has approached the ninety-eight or ninety-nine per cent mark and lists, I hope, everything of importance." Three additional years of bibliographical work, however, have produced scores of new poems, new book reviews, articles, and many new letters-to-the-editor and miscellaneous items, as well as (certainly the most exciting find of all) four new short stories. Taken all together this heretofore undiscovered Nabokoviana would suffice for a neat little volume in itself! So it is that, even though future investigations will almost certainly require great diligence with an ever-diminishing chance of reward, I can only with some hesitancy write in 1972 what I wrote in 1966: this bibliography is still not complete, but I feel that it has approached the ninety-eight or ninety-nine per cent mark and lists, I hope, everything of importance. Because new translations, editions, and reprints of Nabokov now are appearing in a steady stream, a "cut off" date of January, 1972 has been applied.

In conclusion special thanks are due to Prof. Stephen Jan Parker who did extensive work in double-checking my Rul' entries which cost him weeks of altruistic scholarly effort and did much to remove errors from the listings of Nabokov's earliest work, and also to Miss Lyndall Morgan, Prof. Ludmila Foster (compiler of the pioneer Bibliography of Russian Émigré Literature) and Mrs. Natalie Schatz. The degree of help given me by my wife Michele, by Mrs. Nabokov, and especially by my research assistant Helene Crowley has been so great that it could be acknowledged adequately only on the title page.

The user of this bibliography who is himself a bibliographer will of course notice that standard practice for a foreign subject, which would not give translations of titles and first lines, has not been followed. I would hope that the reasons for the inclusion of all the extra translations will be evident enough: the fact that Nabokov is a tri-lingual author, and also the fact that historical chance has determined that for many years at least the people who wish to use this bibliography will have English, not Russian, as a first language.

# A Note on
# the Transliteration

Of the several accepted ways of transliteration, I have chosen a modified version of the Library of Congress system, which, while lacking the European elegance and scholarly austerity of the method used by Nabokov himself, is, I believe, the one most easily understood by most readers.

A. F.

| | | | |
|---|---|---|---|
| a | а | p | п |
| b | б | r | р |
| v | в | s | с |
| g | г | t | т |
| d | д | u | у |
| e | е | f | ф |
| yo | ё | kh | х |
| zh | ж | ts | ц |
| z | з | ch | ч |
| i | и | sh | ш |
| j | й | shch | щ |
| k | к | y | ы |
| l | л | ' | ь |
| m | м | e | э |
| n | н | yu | ю |
| o | о | ya | я |

# Collected
# Poetry

0001     *(Untitled)*. St. Petersburg. Privately printed. 1914
       A verse brochure, non-extant.

0002     **POEMS (STIKHI).** St. Petersburg. Privately printed (500 copies). 1916

0003     *Spring—"The smiles, the sparrows, and the golden spray"* (*Vesna—"Ulybki, vorob'i i bryzgi zolotye"*)

0004     *In Church (V tserkvi)*

0005     *Easter—"The granite of palaces gleamed in the sun"* (*Paskha—"Sverkal na solntse granit dvortsov"*)

0006     *Happiness (Schast'e)*

0007     *"Our boat is almost motionless" ("Pochti nedvizhna nasha lodka")*

0008     *"Carnations call the lover" ("Zovut vlyublyonnogo gvozdiki")*

0009     *"Beyond the forest with a parting smile" ("Za lesom ulybkoj proshchal'noj")*

0010     *"Eternally young are my sorrows" ("Pechali moi vechno molody")*

0011     *"Laughs the color, and laughs the line" ("Smeyotsya kraska, smeyotsya liniya")*

0012     *"No pride and no power has sorrow" ("Pechal' ne sil'na, ne gorda")*

0037 *"The velvet night enveloped us in shadow" ("Nas barkhatnaya noch' okutala tenyami")*

0038 *A Dream (Son)*

0039 *"I recall how obsessively sweet" ("Ya pomnyu, chto byli tomitel'no-sladki")*

0040 *"Hyacinths with their passionate fragrance" ("Giatsinty zapakhom strastnym")*

0041 *Our Star (Nasha zvezda)*

0042 *Lunar Reverie (Lunnaya gryoza)*      0407

0043 *Moonlight (Lunnyj svet)*

0044 *"How the lips burn! Our speeches we bring to an end" ("Kak guby goryat! . . . Dokanchivaem rechi")*

0045 *"You remember my lips growing mute" ("Ty pomnish', kak guby moi onemeli")*

0046 *"That night I could but sob with rapture" ("V tu noch' ya tol'ko mog rydat' ot naslazhden'ya")*

0047 *"The gods of autumn have shrouded the city" ("Okutali gorod osennie bogi")*

0048 *"Over humans that luminous evening was brooding" ("Ètot vecher luchistyj grustil nad lyud'mi")*

0049    *"Softly wept the willows. . . In the misty lake"* (*"Ivy tikho plakali. . . V ozero tumannoe"*)

0050    *"The plucked forget-me-not he carelessly discarded"* (*"Nebrezhno on sorval i brosil nezabudku"*)

0051    *"Beauty! Beauty! In it are mysteriously blended"* (*"Krasota! Krasota! V nej tainstvenno slity"*)

0052    *"There's something I failed to perceive, and there's somewhere a loss"* (*"Ya chto-to ne ponyal i gde-to utrata"*)

0053    *"When in the dark my hand meets yours"* (*"Kogda moya ruka vo t'me tvoyu vstrechaet"*)

0054    *"I want so much, I want so little"* (*"Khochetsya tak mnogo, khochetsya tak malo"*)

0055    English: Translated by A. Field in Nabokov—His Life in Art. Boston. Little, Brown. 1967

0056    *"It happens that clouds race in the blue"* (*"Byvaet, v lazuri begut oblaka"*)

0057    *"Whisper that word to me, that wondrous word"* (*"Shepni mne slovo, to slovo divnoe"*)

0058    *Contrasts (Kontrasty)*

0059    *Two Moments (Dva mgnoven'ya)*

0060    *"Lips tender as sunbeams"* (*"Solnechno-nezhnye gubki"*)

0061     *"Come sit closer to me. We'll remember together"* (*"Syad' poblizhe ko mne. My pripomnim s toboj"*)

0062     *"I shall shed tears at the dread hour of torment"* (*"Ya budu slyozy lit' v tot groznyj chas stradan'ya"*)

0063     *"Chords of music like waves, and the specter of parting"* (*"Akkordy, kak volny i prizrak razluki"*)

0064     *"Enough, farewell! I do not need an answer"* (*"Dovol'no i prosti; otveta mne ne nado"*)

0065     *"How strange to look back after parting"* (*"Mne stranno uvidat' oglyadkoj ot razluki"*)

0066     *"Lilies I want not, innocent white lilies"* (*"Ne nado lilij mne, nevinnykh belykh lilij"*)

0067     *"If sometimes one spends the whole day"* (*"Esli, byvalo, provodish' ves' den'"*)

0068     *"With all my strength I strive to happiness"* (*"Ya stremlyus' vsemi silami k schast'yu"*)

0069     *A Summer Day (Letnij den')*

0070     English: Translated by A. Field in Nabokov—His Life in Art. Boston. Little, Brown. 1967

0071     *"On your threshold I wait, into the future soaring in fancy"* (*"Zhdu na tvoyom poroge, v gryadushchem gryozoj reya"*)

0072 **TWO PATHS. AN ALMANAC (DVA PUTI. AL'MANAKH).** Petrograd. Printer: M. S. Person. 1918
A collection of verse published privately by Nabokov and a Tenishev schoolmate, Andrej Balashov.

0073 *"The dark-blue wallpaper"* (*"Tyomno-sinie oboi"*)

0074 *"The fields float by, the marshes pass"* (*"Plyvut polya, bolota mimo"*)

0075 *Sonnet—"I have returned to my forgotten love"* (*Sonet— "Vernulsya ya kmoej lyubvi zabytoj"*)

0076 *"Rain has flown by and burnt out in its flight"* (*"Dozhd' proletel i sgorel na letu"*)
Written May 1917

0077 English: *The Rain Has Flown.* Translated by Vladimir Nabokov in **Poems and Problems.** *0353*

0078 *"Admiring the tumultuous clouds"* (*"Myatezhnymi lyubuyas' oblakami"*)

0079 *"Dissolved is the thunderstorm, clear the sky"* (*"Groza rastayala. Nebo yasno"*)

0080 *"With rain and wind the birches wrestle"* (*"S dozhdyom i vetrom boryatsya beryozy"*)

0081 *Autumn—"The distance was that day deeper and lighter"* (*Osen'—"Byla v tot den' svetlej i shire dal'"*)

0082 *Sonnet—"A cloudless firmament, and not a sound"* (*Sonet—"Bezoblachnaya vys' i tishina"*)

0083     *"I'm fond of unfamiliar railroad stations"* (*"Ya neznakomye lyublyu voksaly"*)

0084     *"Everlasting terror. The black quagmires."* (*"Vechnyj uzhas. Chyornye tryasiny."*)

0085     *"From the wise and the wicked there's nothing I want"* (*"U mudrykh i zlykh nichego ne proshu"*)

0086     **THE EMPYREAN PATH (GORNIJ PUT').** Berlin. Grani. 1923

0087     *To the Poet (Poètu)*
          Written September 2, 1918

0088     *"Live. Do not murmur, do not number"* (*"Zhivi. Ne zhalujsya, ne chisli"*)
          Written February 14, 1919

0089     *"Vibrate, my faithful verse; hover, remembrance!"* (*"Zveni, moj vernyj stikh, vitaj vospominan'e!"*)
          Written January 31, 1918

0090     *"When from the heavens onto this wild shore"* (*"Kogda s nebes na ètot bereg dikij"*)
          Written February 28, 1918

0091     *An Elegy (Èlegiya)*
          Written January 18, 1919

0092     *Two Ships (Dva korablya)*
          Written March 26, 1918

0093     *"The almonds at the crossroads blossom"* (*"Tsvetyot mindal' na perekryostke"*)

Written March 24, 1918

0094 *"O night, I'm yours! All evil is forgotten" ("O noch', ya tvoj! Vsyo zloe pozabyto")*
   Written April 18, 1918

0095 *"You'll come in and sit down, silent" ("Ty vojdyosh' i molcha syadesh'")*
   Written May 23, 1918

0096 *"Here, in this dacha garden, we were happy" ("Vot dachnyj sad, gde schastlivy my byli")*
   Written May 24, 1918

0097 *Birch Tree in the Vorontsov Park (Beryoza v Vorontsovskom parke)*
   Written April 27, 1918

0098 *Hazel and Birch (Oreshnik i beryoza)*
   Written July 2, 1918

0099 *After the Storm (Posle grozy)*
   Written July 4, 1918

0100 *"What redolence of lime and lilac" ("Kak pakhnet lipoj i siren'yu")*
   Written December 27, 1918

0101 *The Staircase (Lesnitsa)*
   Written July 30, 1918

0102 *"You will forget me as you will this night" ("Zabudesh' ty menya, kak ètu noch zabudesh'")*
   Written August 10, 1918

0113      *"Radiance kindles aloft" ("Razgoraetsya vys'")*
         Written November 11, 1918

0114      *"We were enclosed within a ball of crystal" ("V khrustal'nyj shar zaklyucheny my byli")*

0115      *"If my verse whirls about, if it flies, if it quivers" ("Esli v'yotsya moj stikh i letit i trepeshchet")*
         Written August 23, 1918

0116      *Autumn Dance (Osennyaya plyaska)*
         Written August 8, 1918

0117      *The Little Shoe (Bashmachyok)*
         Written November 20, 1918

0118      *"The cypresses that stand on guard" ("Storozhevye kiparisy")*
         Written November 25, 1918

0119      *"You are asking too much, far too much you are asking!" ("Ty mnogogo, slishkom ty mnogogo khochesh'!")*
         Written November 26, 1918

0120      *The Fairy's Daughter (Feina doch')*
         Written December 1, 1918

0121      *"In the sky you're a delicate cloudlet" ("Ty na nebe oblachko nezhnoe")*
         Written December 10, 1918

0122      *On a Swing (Na kachelyakh)*
         Written December 15, 1918

0123     *The New Year* (*Novyj god*)
       This poem was republished in an émigré tear-off calendar for the date December 31, 1936. Written January 1, 1919

0124     *"Like you, I from my boyhood days"* [to Yu. R.] (*"Kak ty, ya s otrocheskikh dnej"* [Yu. R.])
       Written January, 1919

0125     *Morning* (*Utro*)
       Written February 1, 1919

0126     *"Upon a brilliant cloud reposing"* (*"Na yarkom oblake pokoyas'"*)

0127     *The Scythian* (*Skif*)

0128     *"I have been in the country of Remembrance"* (*"Ya byl v strane vospominan'ya"*)      0436
       Written February 17, 1919

0129     *"Oh the divine thrill of that meeting"* (*"O, vstrechi divnoe volnene"*)

0130     *The Bee*—from the Persian (*Pchela*—s persidskogo)
       Written March 2, 1919

0131     *Peter in Holland* (*Pyotr v Gollandii*)
       Written March 17, 1919

0132     *Russia—"What do I care if a slavegirl or hireling"* (*Rossiya—"Ne vsyo-li ravno mne-raboj li, nayomnitsej"*)      0421
       Written March 5, 1919

0133     *"My love for this life is a frenzied love"* (*"Étu zhizn' ya lyublyu isstuplyonnoj lyubov'yu"*)
        Written March 9, 1919

0134     *Cypresses* (*Kiparisy*)
        Written March 22, 1919

0135     *"Still I am mute, and gaining strength in silence"* (*"Eshchyo bezmolvstvuyu i krepnu ya v tishi"*)
        Written March 23, 1919—n.b. This date is in the old style, whereas the date given by the author (April 4) in **Poems and Problems** has been converted to the new style.

0136     *Istanbul* (*Stambul*)
        Written April 6, 1919

0137     *"You wander about in the garden and brood"* (*"Po sadu brodish' i dumaesh' ty"*)
        Written April 27, 1919

0138     *"What is it that my heart must have"* (*"Chto nuzhno serdtsu moemu"*)
        Written May 5, 1919

0139     *Catkin Week* (*Verba*)
        Written June 26, 1919

0140     *The Water Nymph* (*Rusalka*)        0600
        Written July 13, 1919

0141     *"The clouds have broken up. The diamonds of the rain"* (*"Razbilis' oblaka. Almazy dozhdevye"*)
        Written August 23, 1919

0142 *"So simple my dreaming, so joyful a dream" ("Mne tak prosto i radostno snilos'")*
  Written August 13, 1919

0143 *In Memory of a Friend (Pamyati druga)*

0144 *"A simple song, a simple sadness" ("Prostaya pesnya, grust' prostaya")*
  Written August 17, 1919

0145 *The Blizzard (V'yuga)*        *0409*
  Written August 30, 1919

0146 *"The sky sweeps along, palpitating and blazing" ("Katitsya nebo, dysha i blistaya")*
  Written September 13, 1919

0147 *Autumn—"And again as in those sweet years" (Osen'—"I snova, kak v milye gody")*
  Written September 25, 1919

0148 *"The tower clock sang forth" [to M.W.] ("Chasy na bashne raspevali" [M.W.])*

0149 *"Chimes, and like a dewy rainbow" ("Zvon, i radugoj rosistoj")*
  Written October 12, 1919

0150 *"Be with me more limpid and more simple" ("Bud' so mnoj prozrachnee i proshche")*
  Written November 12, 1919

0151 *Winter—"Only the young firs are stubborn" [to I. A. Bunin] (Zima—"Tol'ko yolochki upryamy" [I. A. Buninu])* *0456*
  Written December 1, 1919

0152 *"My friend, I am sincerely sorry"* (*"Moj drug, ya iskrenne zhaleyu"*)
  Written January 2, 1920

0153 *Spring—"The world is thrilling with a whiff of spring"* (*Vesna—"Vzvolnovan mir vesennim dunoven'em"*)
  Written January 17, 1920

0154 *"The little marchioness knows"* (*"Markiza malen'kaya znaet"*)
  Written January 22, 1920

0155 *Death—"The angels will come out to meet me"* (*Smert'—"Vyjdut angely navstrechu"*)
  Written February 5, 1920

0156 *Drops of Paint* (*Kapli krasok*)
0157 *The All-Forgiving* (*Vseproshchayushchij*)
0158 *Joie de vivre*
0159 *Appletrees* (*Yabloni*)
0160 *Midday in the Crimea* (*Krymskij polden'*)
0161 *Blades of Grass* (*Bylinki*)
0162 *The Artist* (*Khudozhnik*)
0163 *River Lily* (*Rechnaya liliya*)
0164 *In the Forest* (*V lesu*)
0165 *Inspiration* (*Vdokhnoven'e*)
0166 *La morte de Arthur*
0167 *Decadence*
0168 *The Crusaders* (*Krestonostsy*)    *0415*
0169 *A Kimono* (*Kimono*)
0170 *Meretrix*
0171 *Dostoevsky*
0172  English: Translated by A. Field in Nabokov—His Life in Art. Boston. Little, Brown. 1967
0173 *The Airplane—"It slid along the trampled grass"* (*Aèroplan—"Skol'znuv po stoptannoj trave"*)
0174 *Napoleon in Exile* (*Napoleon v izgnanii*)
  Written December 6–24, 1919

0175 *Childhood (Detstvo)*
    Written August 21–22, 1918


0176 *Angels (Angely)*
    Written September 26, 1918
0177 *Seraphim (Serafimy)*
0178 *Cherubim (Kheruvimy)*
    Written September 22, 1918      *0419*
0179 *Thrones (Prestoly)*
    Written September 26, 1918
0180 *Kingdoms (Gospodstva)*
    Written September 26, 1918
0181 *Forces (Sily)*
    Written September 27, 1918
0182 *Powers (Vlasti)*
    Written September 28, 1918
0183 *Beginnings (Nachala)*
    Written September 23, 1919
0184 *Archangels (Arkhangely)*
    Written September 28, 1918
0185 *Guardian Angel (Angel-Khranitel')*


0186 *The Crimea (Krym)*         *0430*
    Written June 30, 1920


0187 *Dream at the Acropolis (Son na Akropole)*
    Written April 25, 1919


0188 *Wanderings (Stranstviya)*      *0421*
    Written February 14, 1920


0189 *"A pale-blueing vapor hangs over the earth" ("Nad zemlyoyu stoit golubeyushchij par")*
    Written February 20, 1920


0190 *Football*
    Written February 26, 1920

0191 *"Lost forever, forever my own"* (*"Bezvozvratnaya, vechno-rodnaya"*)
   Written March 4, 1920


0192 *Motion* (*Dvizhen'e*)
   Written March 9, 1920


0193 *Telegraph Poles* (*Telegrafnye stolby*)


0194 *Chestnut Trees* (*Kashtany*)        *0451*
   Written May 20, 1920


0195 *"In flowing drowsiness I like"* (*"Lyublyu v struyashchejsya dremote"*)


0196 *"I chanced to brush against your airy garments"* (*"Tvoikh odezhd vozdushnykh ya kosnulsya"*)
   Written May 29, 1920. This poem is identified as a fragment.


0197 *Une Romance* (*Romans*)


0198 *Swallows* (*Lastochki*)
   Written June 10, 1920


0199 *Cena Domini* (*Tajnaya Vecherya*)     *0418*
   Written June 12, 1920


0200 *"She has long gone away, she has long since forgotten"* (*"Ona davno ushla, ona davno zabyla"*)


0201 *"I saw you weave amidst the diamond"* [to M. Sh.] (*"Ya videl, ty vitala mezh almaznykh"* [M. Sh.])

0202     *"Who'll be driving me homeward on a rutty road" ("Kto*    0432
           *menya povezyot, po ukhabam, domoj")*
               Written August 8, 1920

0203     *Peacocks (Pavliny)*                                     0415
               Written August 2, 1920. In **The Empyrean Path** this
               poem has an epigraph which it lacks in its first appear-
               ance.

0204     *In Paradise—"Greetings, Death! And my winged compan-*
            *ion" (V rayu—"Zdravstvuj, smert'! i sputnik krylatyj")*
               Written August 13, 1920

0205     *"The ciliary little springs keep ticking" ("Mertsatel'nye*
           *tikayut pruzhinki")*
               Written August 14, 1920

0206     *The Forest (Les)*                                       0444

0207     *The Return (Vozvrashchen'e)*                        0413
               Written October 22, 1920

0208     *The Poet—"Joy and anxiety, he knew" (Poèt—"On znal:*    0432
           *otrada i trevoga")*

0209     *Autumn—"The leaves are falling. Disembodied chimes"*
           *(Osen'—"Vot listopad. Besplotnym perezvonom")*

0210     *Imitation of the Ancients (Podrazhanie drevnim)*
               Written January 19, 1923

0211     *Lawn Tennis*
               Written December 10, 1920

0212       *The Butterfly (Babochka)*

0213       *The Cyclist (Velosipedist)*
          Written September 30, 1918

0214       *"Inspiration is the ardent passion" ("Vdokhnoven'e—èto sladostrast'e")*

0215       *"A monkey in a sarafan" ("Obez'yanu v sarafane")*

0216       *"Armless dwarf in a dress coat" ("Karlik bezrukij vo frake")*
          Written September, 1917

0217       *To an Italian Girl (Ital'yanke)*

0218       *On Calvary (Na Golgofe)*                *0418*

0219       *"My rapture, the clouds and the glittering waters" ("Blazhenstvo moyo, oblaka i blestyashchie vody")*

0220       *"I can't without tears" ("Ya bez slyoz ne mogu")*

0221       *Homewards (Domoj)*

0222       *Birches (Beryozy)*                *0419*

0223       *The Poets—"Well what! In years of din and stench" (Poèty— "Chto-zh! V gody grokhota i smrada")*
          Written July 15, 1919

0224       *Biology*

0225     *"If the wind of fate, for the fun of it"* [to V. Sh.] (*"Esli veter*    0443
*sud'ba, radi shutki"* [V. Sh.])

0226     *The Mendicant Artist (Khudozhnik-nishchij)*

0227     *Clouds (Oblaka)*    0420

0228     *The Feast (Pir)*    0445

0229     *White Paradise (Belyj raj)*    0446

0230     *Horses (Koni)*

0231     *The Mirror (Zerkalo)*

0232     *Night (Noch')*
Written January 30, 1919

0233     *La Belle Dame Sans Merci* [from John Keats]
A translation.  *1290*

0234     *The Drunken Knight (P'yanyj rytsar')*

0235     *"I think of her, that little girl, so distant"* (*"Ya dumayu
o nej, o devochke, o dal'nej"*)

0236     *A Feather (Pero)*    0445

0237     *"In a dim little church we have crowded"* (*"My stolpilis'*    0424
*v tumannoj tserkovenke"*)
There is a minor misspelling in the first line.

0238     *"You'll tell people: the time has now come"* [To my Mother]
       *("Lyudyam ty skazhesh': nastalo"* [Moej materi])
         Written May 3, 1920

0239     *Rus (Rus')*
         Written November 12, 1918

0240     *Life (Zhizn')*

0241     **THE CLUSTER (GROZD').** Berlin. Gamayun. 1923

0242     *"Who will go out at morn? The ripe fruit who will notice?"*     *0451*
       *("Kto vyjdet poutru? Kto spelyj plod podmetit?")*

0243     *"Weighed down by stifling drowsiness" ("Pridavlen*
       *dushnoyu dremotoj")*

0244     *"There's liberty in solitude" ("Est' v odinochestve svoboda")*

0245     English: Translated by A. Field in Nabokov—His Life in
       Art. Boston. Little, Brown. 1967

0246     *"From shine to shade, from shade to shine" ("Iz bleska v*
       *ten', i v blesk iz teni")*

0247     *"I'm looking seaward from a marble temple" ("Ya na more*
       *glyazhu iz mramornogo khrama")*

0248     *"Mists of night sleep, coating of dusty languor" ("Tuman*
       *nochnogo sna, nalyot istomy pyl'noj")*

0249     *"A maple leaf upon black velvet" ("Na chyornyj barkhat*     *0438*
       *list klenovyj")*

0250      *"We, the young ones, the winged, are few"* (*"Nas malo— yunykh, okrylyonnykh"*)      *0446*

0251      *On the Anniversary of Dostoevsky's Death* (*Na godov-shchinu smerti Dostoevskogo*)      *0434*

0252      *On the Death of Blok—"Mists after mists floated by"* (*Na smert' Bloka—"Za tumanami plyli tumany"*)
In the printing of two poems on Blok in this edition the title Na smert' Bloka should not have been itali-cized and a Roman numeral should have been placed above the first poem. The poems did appear separately in The Rudder. See *0427* and *0431*.

0253      *"Like mountain streams your voice is proud and clear"* [To Ivan Bunin] (*"Kak vody gor, tvoj golos gord i chist"* [Ivanu Buninu])      *0411*

0254      *"When, still bedimmed, we saw each other first"* (*"Kogda, tumannye, my svidelis' vpervye"*)

0255      *"About you I daydreamed so long ago, so often"* (*"Mechtal ya o tebe tak chasto, tak davno"*)

0256      *Sonnet—"A spring-time wood I see in fancy. Wait"* (*Sonet— "Vesennyj les mne chuditsya. . . Postoj"*)      *0453*

0257      *"Let me daydream. You're my first anguish"* (*"Pozvol' mechtat'. Ty pervoe stradan'e"*)

0258      *"Her soul, like an extraordinary light"* (*"Eyo dusha, kak svet neobychajnyj"*)

0259      *"When you'll wish it I shall leave"* (*"Kogda zakhochesh', ya ujdu"*)

0260     *"O bright voice, slightly tinged with sadness"* *("O, svetlyj golos, chut' pechal'nyj")*

0261     *"All the windows you opened, the curtains you drew"* *("Vse okna otkryv, opustiv zanaveski")*

0262     *"At full moon, in the drawing room, dusty and sumptuous"* *("V polnolun'e, v gostinoj pyl'noj i pyshnoj")*

0263     *"O love, you are bright, you are winged"* *("O, lyubov', ty svetla i krylata")*

0264     *Eyes (Glaza)*

0265     *"However dismally and densely"* *("Puskaj vsyo gorestnej i glushe")*       *0455*

0266     *Easter—"I see a shining cloud, a roof"* *(Paskha—"Ya vizhu oblako siyayushchee, kryshu")*

0267     *"Be silent, don't stir up your soul"* *("Molchi, ne vspenivaj dushi")*       *0445*

0268     *Tristram (Tristan)*       *0441*

0269     *"You see my signet ring? For stars, for precious stones"* *("Ty vidish' persten' moj? Za zvyozdy, za kamen'ya")*

0270     *"All I recall is piny fragrance"* *("Ya pomnyu tol'ko dukh sosnovyj")*

0271     *Christmas (Rozhdestvo)*

0272      *At a Village Cemetery (Na sel'skom kladbishche)*

0273      *Viola Tricolor*                                                    *0428*

0274      *In the Menagerie (V zverintse)*

0275      *Moths (Nochnye babochki)*                                          *0448*

0276      *In the Train (V poezde)*                                           *0425*

0277      *The Express (Ėkspress)*

0278      *"How often, how often in a fast train" ("Kak chasto, kak
          chasto ya v poezde skorom")*

0279      **THE RETURN OF CHORB: STORIES AND POEMS
          (VOZVRASHCHENIE CHORBA: RASSKAZY I STIKHI).** Berlin.
          Slovo. 1930. 246 pp.
            See short stories listing. *0678*

0280      *"For happiness the man in love can't sleep" ("Ot schastiya
          vlyublyonnomu ne spitsya")*

0281      *Soft Sound (Tikhij shum)*                                         *0531*
            Written in early 1929

0282      *Bricks (Kirpichi)*                                                *0556*

0283      *The Mailbox (Pochtovyj yashchik)*

0284      *An Enchanting Season (Prelestnaya pora)*                          *0538*

*0299*  *Dreams (Sny)*  *0537*

*0300*  *The Room (Komnata)*  *0535*

*0301*  *The Mother (Mat')*  *0514*

*0302*  *Spring—"Off to the country puffs the train" (Vesna—* *0516*
*"Pomchal na dachu parovoz")*

*0303*  *In Paradise (V rayu)*  *0552*

Reprinted in Facets (Grani). Munich. October–
December 1959

*0304*  English: *In Paradise*. Translated by A. Field in
Nabokov—His Life in Art. Boston. Little, Brown. 1967

*0305*  *In Paradise*. Translated by Vladimir Nabokov in **Poems
and Problems.**  *0353.*

*0306*  **POEMS 1929–1951 (STIKHOTVORENIYA 1929–1951).** Paris.
Rifma. 1952. 45pp.
Author's note: "The poems selected for this edition were
composed in Germany, France, and America between
1929 and 1951. The first of them concludes the period
of my youthful art. The poems presented here were
published in émigré journals and newspapers, and nine
of them appeared under pseudonyms: 'V. Sirin' (the first
seven) and 'Vasilij Shishkov' (the following two)."

*0307*  Italy: **Poesie.** Translated by Alberto Pescetto and Enzo
Siciliano. Milan. Il Saggiatore. 1962
This book is composed of sixteen Russian poems from
**Poems 1929–1951,** translated by Alberto Pescetto, and
fourteen English poems from the 1959 **Poems,** translated by Enzo Siciliano, all with facing texts. The
27

translations are also listed with their Italian titles or first lines under Poems—Separate Appearances.

0308      *"Your coming I recall: a growing vibrance"* (*"Ya pomnyu tvoj prikhod: rastushchij zvon"*)
This poem, written in 1929, appeared in this collection for the first time.

Reprinted in Facets (Grani). Munich. October–December 1959

0309      Italy: *"Ricordo il tuo arrivo: uno squillo crescente"*. Translated by Alberto Pescetto in Poesie. *0307*

0310      *Evening on a Vacant Lot* (*Vecher na pustyre*)      *0580*

0311      *How I Love You* (*Kak ya lyublyu tebya*)      *0586*

0312      *"At sunset, by the same bench"* (*"Na zakate, u toj zhe skam'i"*)

0313      English: *At Sunset.* Translated by Vladimir Nabokov in **Poems and Problems.** *0353*

0314      Italy: *"In un tramonto, accanto alla medesima panca"*. Translated by Alberto Pescetto in Poesie. *0307*

0315      *L'inconnue de la Seine*      *0589*
The first line rather than the title of this poem was used in the table of contents through a printer's error.

0316      *"What happened overnight to memory?"* (*"Chto za-noch' s pamyat'yu sluchilos'?"*)

0317      English: *What Happened Overnight*. Translated by Vladimir Nabokov in **Poems and Problems.** *0353*

0318      Italy: *"Che cosa accadde alla memoria nella notte?"*. Translated by Alberto Pescetto in Poesie. *0307*

0319      *"We so firmly believed in the linkage of life"* (*"My s toboyu tak verili v svyaz' bytiya"*)

0320      Reprinted in Facets (Grani). Munich. October–December 1959

0321      English: *We So Firmly Believed*. Translated by Vladimir Nabokov in **Poems and Problems.** *0353*

0322      Italy: *"Noi credevamo tanto nel vincolo dell'esistenza"*. Translated by Alberto Pescetto in Poesie. *0307*

0323      *The Poets* (*Poèty*)

           Reprinted in Facets (Grani). Munich. October–December 1959

           Reprinted in Tri-Quarterly. Evanston, Illinois. No. 17. Winter 1970. In both Russian and English.

0324      English: Translated by Vladimir Nabokov in **Poems and Problems.** *0353*

0325      Italy: *Poeti*. Translated by Alberto Pescetto in Poesie. *0307*

0326      *"Will you leave me alone, I implore you!"* (*"Otvyazhis'—ya tebya umolyayu!"*)    *0591*

0327  *Fame (Slava)*             *0601*

0328  *A Parisian Poem (Parizhskaya poèma)*    *0609*

0329  *"No matter in what battle piece depicted" ("Kakim by*  *0612*
    *polotnom batal'nym ni yavlyalas' ")*

0330  English: Translated by Vladimir Nabokov, with facing
    Russian text, in Modern Russian Poetry edited by V.
    Markov and M. Sparks. London. MacGibbon & Kee.
    1966

0331  *On Rulers (O pravitelyakh)*       *0616*

0332  *To Prince S. M. Kachurin (K kn. S. M. Kachurinu)*  *0620*

0333  *"A day like any other. Memory dozed" ("Byl den' kak den'.*  *0403*
    *Dremala pamyat'. Dlilas' ")*
    Written in 1951

0334  English: *A Day Like Any Other.* Translated by Vladimir  *0403*
    Nabokov in **Poems and Problems.** *0353*

0335  **POEMS.** New York. Doubleday. 1959; and London. Weiden-
    feld & Nicolson. 1961
    With one Russian exception (a poem from the novel **The
    Gift**), all the poems which are read by Vladimir Nabokov
    on Lolita and Poems (Spoken Arts Recording 902) are
    from this volume.

0336  *The Refrigerator Awakes*        *0597*

0337  *A Literary Dinner*          *0595*

| | | |
|---|---|---|
| *0338* | *A Discovery* | |
| *0339* | *The Poem* | |
| *0340* | *An Eve ing of Russian Poetry* | *0614* |
| *0341* | *The Room* | *0623* |
| *0342* | *Voluptates tactionum* | *0625* |

*0343*  *Restoration*
This poem first appeared in this collection.

*0344*  Italy: *Restuaro*. Translated by Enzo Siciliano in Poesie. *0307*

*0345*  *The Poplar*
The initial appearance of this poem in an American journal is unlocated.

*0346*  Italy: *Il pioppo*. Translated by Enzo Siciliano in Poesie. *0307*

| | | |
|---|---|---|
| *0347* | *Lines Written in Oregon* | *0627* |
| *0348* | *Ode to a Model* | *0633* |
| *0349* | *On Translating* | |
| *0350* | *Rain* | *0635* |

| 0351 | *The Ballad of Longwood Glen* | *0638* |
|------|-------------------------------|--------|

*0351A*     Excerpts from **Poems** included in The New Yorker Book of Poems. New York. Viking. 1969; and London. Macmillan. 1969

> Five poems (*The Ballad of Longwood Glen, An Evening of Russian Poetry, Lines Written in Oregon, On Discovering a Butterfly* and *The Room*), all of which initially appeared in The New Yorker, are anthologized here.

*0352*     NABOKOV's CONGERIES and THE PORTABLE NABOKOV

> For poems reprinted in these volumes see *1242*.

*0353*     **POEMS AND PROBLEMS.** New York. McGraw-Hill. 1971; and London. Weidenfeld & Nicolson. 1971

> This volume contains dual language texts for all the poems written in Russian, English poems, and also a selection of chess problems published over the years. In the listing of Russian poems with their translations the English version comes first for the sake of bibliographic uniformity although in **Poems and Problems** itself the Russian poems precede the translation. Nabokov's own system of transliteration, differing from the one used throughout this bibliography, has been retained here as it is used in the table of contents.

| *0354* | *A Literary Dinner* | *0595* |
|--------|---------------------|--------|

| *0355* | *The Refrigerator Awakes* | *0597* |
|--------|---------------------------|--------|

| *0356* | *A Discovery* | |
|--------|---------------|--|

| *0357* | *The Poem* | |
|--------|------------|--|

| *0358* | *An Evening of Russian Poetry* | *0614* |
|--------|-------------------------------|--------|

0371    *Hotel Room* and the Russian original *Nomer v gostinitse*
This poem, written on April 8, 1919, a few days before
the young Nabokov left Russia, is published here for
the first time.

0372    *Provence* and the Russian original *Provans*                    *0477*
This constitutes half of a longer poem, of which this
half appears under a different title in The Rudder in
1923.

0373    *La Bonne Lorraine*                                              *0501*

0374    *The Blazon* and the Russian original *Gerb*                     *0512*

0375    *The Mother* and the Russian original *Mat'*                     *0514*

0376    *I Like That Mountain* and the Russian original *Lyublyu*        *0525*
    *ya goru*

0377    *The Dream* and the Russian original *Snovidenie*               *0542*

0378    *The Snapshot* and the Russian original *Snimok*               *0545*

0379    *In Paradise* and the Russian original *V rayu*                 *0552*

0380    *The Execution* and the Russian original *Rasstrel*            *0549*

0381    *For Happiness the Lover Cannot Sleep* and the Russian         *0559*
    original *Ot schastiya vlyublyonnomu ne spitsya*

0382    *Lilith* and the Russian original *Lilit*
This poem, written in 1928, is published here for the
first time.

# Poems:
## Separate Appearances

0407    *Lunar Reverie* (*Lunnaya gryoza*) in The Messenger of Europe (Vestnik Evropy). St. Petersburg. July 1916. pg. 39

0408    *Winter Night* (*Zimnyaya noch'*) in Russian Thought (Russkaya Mysl'). St. Petersburg. March–April 1917

0409    *Requiem* (*Panikhida*); *The Blizzard* (*V'yuga*); *After the Storm* (*Posle grozy*) in The Future of Russia (Gryadushchaya Rossiya). Paris. January 1920
        *Requiem* was reprinted in Native Land (Rodnaya zemlya). New York. 1920. This poem was signed V. V. Nabokov.

0410    *"How alluring my North is in Spring"* (*"Kak vesnoyu moj sever prizyven"*) in The Rudder (Rul'). Berlin. April 10, 1920?
        The exact date of this poem is very much in doubt as this manuscript goes to press. See *0467*.

0411    *"Like mountain streams your voice is proud and clear"* [To I. A. Bunin] (*"Kak vody gor, tvoj golos gord i chist"* [I. A. Buninu] in The Rudder (Rul'). Berlin. October 1, 1920)
        *I. A. Buninu* was used as the title of this poem rather than as a mere dedication.

0412    *Home* in The Trinity Magazine. No. 5. Vol. 2. Cambridge. November 1920. pg. 16

0413    *The Return* (*Vozvrashchenie*) in The Rudder (Rul'). Berlin. December 10, 1920. pg. 3

0414    *Remembrance* in The English Review. London. 1920. pg. 392

0415　　　　*Apocrypha (Skazaniya); The Apparition to Joseph (Videnie Iosifa); The Crusaders (Krestonostsy); Peacocks (Pavliny)* in The Rudder (Rul'). Berlin. January 7, 1921. pg. 2

0416　　　　*Quiet Autumn (Tikhaya osen')* in The Rudder (Rul'). Berlin. February 20, 1921. pg. 2

0417　　　　*Spring—"Where are you, little wind of April" (Vesna— "Gde ty, aprelya veterok")* in The Rudder (Rul'). Berlin. April 12, 1921. pg. 2
　　　　　　The poem appeared in The Rudder in two stanzas, the second of which (*"I can't look at you, Spring, without tears"*) appears as a separate poem in **The Empyrean Path.** *0086*

0418　　　　*Cena Domini (Tajnaya Vecherya); On Calvary (Na Golgofe)* in The Rudder (Rul'). Berlin. April 29, 1921. pg. 2

0419　　　　*Cherubim (Kheruvimy); Birches (Beryozy); My Spring (Moya Vesna)* in The Rudder (Rul'). Berlin. May 1, 1921. pg. 2
　　　　　　A misprint in *Birches* was corrected in **The Empyrean Path.** *0086*

0420　　　　*Clouds (Oblaka)* in The Rudder (Rul'). Berlin. May 22, 1921

0421　　　　*Wanderings (Stranstviya); Russia—"What do I care if a slavegirl or hireling" (Rossiya—"Ne vsyo li ravno mne—raboj-li, nayomnitsej")* in Russian Thought (Russkaya Mysl'). Sofia. V–VII (May–July), 1921. pp. 76–77

0422　　　　*The Exiles (Bezhentsy)* in The Rudder (Rul'). Berlin. May ?, 1921

　　　　　　Reprinted in An Anthology of Satire and Humor (Antologiya Satiry i Yumora). Berlin. 1222

0423     Russian poem in The Rudder (Rul'). Berlin. June 19, 1921. pg. 2

A Sirin poem is listed in the front page index of this issue of The Rudder, but unfortunately pg. 2 is missing from the microfilm run examined and so the poem cannot be identified.

0424     *"In the dim little church we have crowded"* (*"My stolpilis' v tumannoj tserkovenke"*) in The Rudder (Rul'). Berlin. June 29, 1921. pg. 2

0425     *In the Train* (*V poezde*) in The Rudder (Rul'). Berlin. July 10, 1921. pg. 2

0426     *Petersburg—"So here it is, the former wizard"* (*Peterburg—"Tak vot on, prezhnij charodej"*) in The Rudder (Rul'). Berlin. July 17, 1921. pg. 2

Reprinted in St. Petersburg in the Poems of Russian Poets (Peterburg v Stikhotvoreniyakh Russkikh Poètov), edited by G. Alekseev. Berlin. Severnye Ogni. 1923. pp. 81–85

0427     *On the Death of A. Blok—"Mists after mists floated by"* (*Na Smert' A. Bloka—"Za tumanami plyli tumany"*) in The Rudder (Rul'). Berlin. August 14, 1921. pg. 2

This appearance contains a typographical error corrected in **The Cluster.** *0241*

0428     *Viola Tricolor* in The Rudder (Rul'). Berlin. August 21, 1921. pg. 5

0429     Russian poem in Today (Segodnya). Riga. August 30, 1921

The text of this poem has not been located.

0430     *The Crimea* (*Krym*) in The Fire-Bird (Zhar-Ptitsa). No. 1. Berlin. August 1921. pp. 36–37

0431    *On the Death of Blok—"Pushkin, rainbow over all the earth" (Na smert' Bloka—"Pushkin-raduga po vsej zemle")* in The Rudder (Rul'). Berlin. September 20, 1921. pg. 4

0432    *Autumn—"The leaves are falling. Disembodied chimes" (Osen'—"Vot listopad. Besplotnym perezvonom"); "Who'll be driving me homeward on a rutty road" ("Kto menya povezyot, po ukhabam, domoj"); The Reversion (Vozvrat)* in The Rudder (Rul'). Berlin. October 2, 1921. pg. 7

0433    *"While in the mist of dubious days" ("Poka v tumane strannykh dnej"); "How long since o'er the snowy quay" ("Davnol' po naberezhnoj snezhnoj")* in Contemporary Annals (Sovremennye Zapiski). No. 7. Paris. October 5, 1921. pp. 107–108

0434    *A Legend (from the Apocrypha) (Skazanie [iz apokrifa])* in The Rudder (Rul'). Berlin. November 11, 1921. pg. 4
    *This poem appears in* **The Cluster** *under the title On the Anniversary of Dostoevsky's Death.* 0251

0435    *The Acropolis (Akropol')* in The Rudder (Rul'). Berlin. November 13, 1921. pg. 2

0436    *In Egypt (V Egipte)* in The Rudder (Rul'). Berlin. November 23, 1921. pg. 4
    *This poem ("I have been in the country of Remembrance") was reprinted without the title in* **The Empyrean Path.** 0128

0437    *The Shrine (Khram)* in The Rudder (Rul'). Berlin. December 4, 1921. pg. 2

0438    *Autumn Leaves (Osennie list'ya): "A blind man is playing his violin at the corner" ("V pereulke na skripke igraet slepoy"); "A maple leaf upon black velvet" ("Na chyornyi barkhat list' klenovyj"); "I'm standing on the porch. Across the street there dwells" ("Stoyu ya na kryl'tse. Naprotiv obitaet")* in The Rudder (Rul'). Berlin. December 7, 1921. pg. 3

0439    *By the Fireplace (U kamina); "A simple song, a simple sadness" ("Prostaya pesnya, grust' prostaya"); Night (Noch')* in The Rudder (Rul'). Berlin. December 22, 1921. pg. 4

0440    *A Feather (Pero)* in The Fire-Bird (Zhar-Ptitsa). Nos. 4–5. Berlin. 1921. pg. 40

0441    *Tristram (Tristan)* in Northern Lights (Spolokhi). No. 1. Berlin. 1921

0442    *My Calendar (Moj kalendar')* in Northern Lights (Spolokhi). No. 2. Berlin. 1921

0443    *"If the wind of fate for the fun of it" ("Esli veter sud'ba radi shutki")* in The Rudder (Rul'). Berlin. 1921?

0444    *The Forest (Les)* in The Rudder (Rul'). Berlin. 1921?
        This poem, for which a more precise date has not been found, is signed Cantab.

0445    *The Feast (Pir)* in The Rudder (Rul'). Berlin. January 7, 1922. pg. 2

0446    *"We, the young ones, the winged, are few" ("Nas malo— yunykh, okrylyonnykh"); White Paradise (Belyj raj); The Ring (Persten')* in The Rudder (Rul'). Berlin. January 29, 1922. pg. 2

0447    *"O night, I am yours! All evil is forgotten"* (*"O noch', ya tvoj! Vsyo zloe pozabyto"*) in The Rudder (Rul'). Berlin. February 15, 1922. pg. 2

0448    *Moths* (*Nochnye babochki*) in The Rudder (Rul'). Berlin. March 15, 1922. pg. 2
        A long poem.

0449    *Easter* (*Paskha*) in The Rudder (Rul'). Berlin. April 16, 1922. pg. 10

0450    *The Prompter* (*Suflyor*) in Theater and Life (Teatr i Zhizn'). No. 10. Berlin. May 1922. pg. 6

0451    *Chestnut Trees* (*Kashtany*); *"Who will go out at morn? The ripe fruit who will notice?"* (*"Kto vyjdet poutru? Kto spelyj plod podmetit?"*) in The Rudder (Rul'). Berlin. June 4, 1922. pg. 2

0452    *"Is my faith known to you?"* (*"Znaesh' veru moyu"*) in The Rudder (Rul'). Berlin. June 22, 1922

0453    *Sonnet—"A spring-time wood I see in fancy. Wait"* (*Sonet—"Vesennyj les mne chuditsya . . . Postoj"*) in The Rudder (Rul'). Berlin. June 25, 1922. pg. 2

0454    *St. Petersburg—"It was constructed on a quagmire"* (*Peterburg—"On na tryasine byl postroen"*) in Russian Thought (Russkaya Mysl'). Prague. VI–VII (July–August), 1922. pg. 57

0455    *"However dismally and densely"* (*"Puskaj vsyo gorestnej i glushe"*); *"Be silent, don't stir up your soul"* (*"Molchi, ne vspenivaj dushi"*) in The Rudder (Rul'). Berlin. August 22, 1922

0456    *Winter—"Only the young firs are stubborn"* [To I. A.
        Bunin] (*Zima—"Tol'ko yolochki upryamy"* [I. A. Buninu])
        in The Rudder (Rul'). Berlin. September ?, 1922


0457    *Mushrooms (Griby); At a Village Cemetery (Na sel'skom
        kladbishche)* in The Rudder (Rul'). Berlin. November 19,
        1922. pg. 2


0458    *Russia (Rossiya)* in Contemporary Annals (Sovremennye
        Zapiski). No. 11. Paris. November 1922. pp. 142–143
        Written November 11, 1918


0459    *A Snowy Night (Snezhnaya noch'); The Knight's Betrothed
        (Nevesta rytsarya)* in The Rudder (Rul'). Berlin. Decem-
        ber 3, 1922. pg. 2


0460    *The Beetle (Zhuk)* in The Rudder (Rul'). Berlin. December
        17, 1922. pg. 2


0461    *The Legend of the Old Woman in Search of a Carpenter
        (Legenda o starukhe, iskavshej plotnika)* in The Rudder
        (Rul'). Berlin. December 24, 1922. pg. 2


0462    *Spring—"Again, again the world dreams of you"
        (Vesna—"Ty snish'sya miru snova, snova")* in The Fire-
        Bird (Zhar-Ptitsa). No. 7. Berlin. 1922. pg. 2


0463    *"We'll be back, it's been pledged by the spring" ("My
        vernyomsya, vesna obeshchala"); "The lips of Earth, the
        beautiful and great" ("Usta zemli velikoj i prekrasnoj");
        "Night ranges o'er the fields and every blade of grass"
        ("Noch' brodit po polyam i kazhduyu bylinku"); "The
        wandering winds whisper to me" ("Shepchut mne
        stranniki vetry")* included in The Spindle, Book One
        (Vereteno, kniga pervaya). Berlin. Otto Kirchner. 1922

0464     *The Penguin (Pingvin); "I dream that I'm a dwarf" ("Mne snitsya: karlik ya"); The Fairy's Daughter (Feina doch')* included in Rainbow (Raduga) edited by S. Chyorny. Berlin. Slovo. 1922
*"I dream that I'm a dwarf"* was written June 1917.

0465     *Metres* [To Gleb Struve] (*Razmery* [Glebu Struve]) in Russian Thought (Russkaya Mysl'). Prague-Berlin. I–II (January–February), 1923. pg. 117

0466     *"I'm somewhere in suburban fields" ("Ya gde-to za gorodom, v pole")* in The Rudder (Rul'). Berlin. February 27, 1923
Written January 20, 1923

0467     *Native Land—"How alluring my North is in the Spring!" (Rodina—"Kak vesnoyu moj sever prizyven!")* in The Rudder (Rul'). Berlin. Late March–April, 1923
The exact date of this poem has not been established (see *0410*), but it should not be confused with *To My Native Land* (below) nor with another poem entitled *Native Land* that appears in September or *To My Native Land* published in 1924. The second portion of this *Native Land* (*"Lost forever, forever my own"*) appears as a separate poem in **The Empyrean Path.** *0191*

0468     *A Dream—"You know, you know as in a drunken swoon" (Son—"Znaesh', znaesh': obmorochno-p'yano")* in Russian Thought (Russkaya Mysl'). Prague-Berlin. III–V (March–May), 1923. pg. 136

0469     *To My Native Land—"Advancing with a cooing warmth, the sixth" (Rodine—"Vorkuyushcheyu teplotoj shestaya")* in The Rudder (Rul'). Berlin. April 8, 1923. pg. 5
Written March 31, 1923

0470     *"When I, up a diamond staircase" ("Kogda ya po lesnitse almaznoj")* in The Rudder (Rul'). Berlin. April 29, 1923

Written April 21, 1923. pg. 2

0471    *Hexameters (Gekzametry)* including *The Miracle (Chudo)*;
        *St. Joseph's Spectacles (Ochki Iosifa)*; *The Heart
        (Serdtse)*; *In Memory of Gumilyov (Pamyati Gumilyova)*
        in The Rudder (Rul'). Berlin. May 6, 1923. pg. 2
        *The Heart* was written March 29, 1923; *In Memory of
        Gumilyov*, March 19, 1923

0472    *The Panther (Bars)* in The Rudder (Rul'). Berlin. May 10,
        1923. pg. 2

0473    *The Storm (Groza)* in The Rudder (Rul'). Berlin. June 10,
        1923. pg. 2

0474    *The Meeting (Vstrecha)* in The Rudder (Rul'). Berlin. June
        24, 1923. pg. 2
        This poem has an epigraph from Blok.

0475    *Poems—"Live on, reverb, don't mention miracles"
        (Stikhotvoreniya—"Zhivi, zvuchi, ne pominaj o chude");
        "O, how you strain to wing your way" ("O, kak ty
        rvyosh'sya v put' krylatyj"); "Out of an inky cloud you
        keep on peering" ("Ty vsyo glyadish' iz tuchi tyomno-
        sizoj")* in Russian Thought (Russkaya Mysl'). Prague-
        Berlin. VI–VIII (June–August), 1923. pp. 11–12

0476    *A Song (Pesnya)* in The Rudder (Rul'). Berlin. July 29, 1923.
        pg. 2

0477    *Provence (Provans): "How avidly holding one's breath"
        ("Kak zhadno zataya dykhan'e"); "I wander aimlessly
        from lane to lane" ("Slonyayus' pereulkami bez tseli")*
        in The Rudder (Rul'). Berlin. September 2, 1923. pg. 2
        Written August 19, 1923

Included in Russian Grammar by F. A. Lyatski. Prague.
1927

0478     English: *Provence*. Translated by Vladimir Nabokov in
**Poems and Problems.** *0353*
Only the second half of this poem appears in **Poems
and Problems.** In addition this second portion appears
under the title *Sun* (*Solntse*) in **The Return of Chorb,**
to which appearance there is a muddled reference in
the bibliography to **Poems and Problems.**

0479     *My Native Land—"When from our native land there
rings" (Rodina—"Kogda iz rodiny zvenit nam")* The
*Deer* (*Olen'*) in The Rudder (Rul'). Berlin. September 23,
1923. pg. 8

0480     *Yuletide* (*Svyatki*) in The Rudder (Rul'). Berlin. December?,
1923; and Russian Echo (Russkoe Èkho). Berlin. Decem-
ber?, 1923.
This poem appeared, through the author's error, in
both newspapers; subsequently it was reprinted with
a different first stanza. The precise date of publication
for either paper has not yet been determined.

0481     *"And those who've come from Earth to Paradise" ("I v
Bozhij raj prishedshie s zemli")* in The Fire-Bird (Zhar-
Ptitsa). No. 11. Berlin. 1923. pg. 32

0482     *The Bonfire* (*Kostyor*) in The Gallipoli Messenger (Gal-
lipoliiskij Vestnik). Sofia. 1923

0483     *The Apparition* (*Videnie*) in The Rudder (Rul'). Berlin.
January 27, 1924. pg. 2

0484     *The Wanderers* (*Skital'tsy*) in The Rudder (Rul'). Berlin.
March 2, 1924. pg. 2

0485    *Cubes (Kuby)* in The Rudder (Rul'). Berlin. March 9, 1924. pg. 2

0486    *The Window (Okno)* in The Rudder (Rul'). Berlin. March 23, 1924. pg. 2

        Reprinted in The Week (Nedelya). Paris. May 5, 1930?

0487    *Leningrad; The Charade (Sharada)* in Our World (Nash mir). Berlin. March 23, 1924

0488    *Poem—"While wandering in an untended garden" (Stikhi— "Bluzhdaya po zapushchennomu sadu")* in The Rudder (Rul'). Berlin. April 3, 1924. pg. 2

0489    *Stanzas (Stansy)* in The Rudder (Rul'). Berlin. April 18, 1924. pg. 2

0490    *An Automobile in the Mountains—A Sonnet (Avtomobil' v gorakh—Sonet)* in The Rudder (Rul'). Berlin. April 20, 1924. pg. 2

0491    *The Boxer's Girl (Podruga boksyora)* in Our World (Nash mir). Berlin. May 11, 1924. pp. 1–2

0492    *Saint Petersburg—"Come, Leila, misty one, to me!" (Sankt Peterburg—"Ko mne, tumannaya Leila!")* in The Rudder (Rul'). Berlin. June 1, 1924. pg. 2

0493    *The Death of Pushkin (Smert' Pushkina)* in Russian Echo (Russkoe Ėkho). Berlin. June 8, 1924. pg. 4

0494    *Death—"The avid hum of life will cease" (Smert'— "Utikhnet zhizni rokot zhadnyj")* in The Rudder (Rul'). Berlin. June 18, 1924. pg. 2

0495    *The Guest (Gost')* in The Rudder (Rul'). Berlin. July 6, 1924. pg. 2

0496    *On Angels—"An unearthly sunrise"; "Imagine we met him" (Ob angelakh—"Nezemnoj rassvet"; "Predstav', my ego vstrechaem")* in The Rudder (Rul'). Berlin. July 20, 1924. pg. 2

0497    *Prayer (Molitva)* in The Rudder (Rul'). Berlin. August 24, 1924. pg. 2

0498    *St. Petersburg—Three sonnets (Peterburg—tri soneta): "There is one path and a great many roads" ("Edinyj put' i mnozhestvo dorog"); "I am tormented by lost days" ("Terzaem ya utrachennymi dnyami"); "The past has wafted back . . . I am alive" ("Poveyalo proshedshim—ya zhivu")* in Russian Echo (Russkoe Èkho). Berlin. August 24, 1924. pg. 8

0499    *Fortune-telling (Gadan'e)* in Today (Segodnya). Riga. August 26, 1924. pg. 11. Also in Russian Echo (Russkoe Èkho). Berlin. December 21, 1924

0500    *The Russian River (Russkaya reka)* in Our World (Nash mir). Berlin. September 14, 1924
By the author's whim this poem was set as a prose piece.

0501    *La Bonne Lorraine* in The Rudder (Rul'). Berlin. September 16, 1924. pg. 2

0502    *English: La Bonne Lorraine.* Translated by Vladimir Nabokov in **Poems and Problems.** *0353*

0503    *Exodus (Iskhod)* in The Rudder (Rul'). Berlin. October 26, 1924. pg. 2

0504  *Three Chess Sonnets (Tri shakhmatnykh soneta)*: *"In the rook's moves there is iambic measure"* (*"V khodakh lad'i—yambicheskij razmer"*); *"Movements of rhyme and of winged dancing girls"* (*"Dvizhen'ya rifm i tantsov-shchits krylatykh"*); *"I did not write a sonnet as pre-scribed"* (*"Ya ne pisal zakonnogo soneta"*) in Our World (Nash mir). Berlin. November 30, 1924. pg. 1

0505  *The Land of Poems (Strana stikhov)* in The Rudder (Rul'). Berlin. December 7, 1924. pg. 2

0506  *"And the funereal . . ."* (*"I traurnye . . ."*) in Russian Echo (Russkoe Èkho). Berlin. No. 12. December 21, 1924.
    The end of this first line, taken from faulty microfilm, is missing.

0507  *The Snowman (Velikan)* in Today (Segodnya). Riga. December 25, 1924. pg. 5

0508  *To My Native Land—"Night is given to reflect and smoke"* (*K rodine—"Noch' dana, chtob dumat' i kurit'"*) in The Rudder (Rul'). Berlin. December 25, 1924. pg. 2

0509  *Christmas Verse (Rozhdestvenskie stikhi): The Wolf Cub (Volchyonok); The Lamb (Ovtsa)* in Our World (Nash mir). Berlin. January 4, 1925. pg. 1

0510  *The Skater (Kon'kobezhets)* in The Rudder (Rul'). Berlin. February 5, 1925. pg. 2

0511  *The Blazon (Gerb)* in Russian Echo (Russkoe Èkho). Berlin. March 1, 1925.
    Written January 4, 1925. In the bibliography to **Poems and Problems,** Nabokov himself lists the publication date of this poem as March 3, but this date is in error. This poem, now translated by Nabokov as *The Blazon,* has been referred to in print as *The Coat of Arms.*

0512    English: *The Blazon*. Translated by Vladimir Nabokov in **Poems and Problems.** *0353*

0513    *Easter Rain (Paskhal'nyj dozhd')* in Russian Echo (Russkoe Èkho). No. 15. Berlin. March 29?, 1925

0514    *The Mother (Mat')* in Russian Echo (Russkoe Èkho). No. 16. Berlin. April 19, 1925. Also in The Rudder (Rul'). Berlin. April 19, 1925. pg. 2

0515    English: *The Mother*. Translated by Vladimir Nabokov in **Poems and Problems.** *0353*
        In the bibliography to this volume Nabokov lists the publication dates for the poem in both Russian Echo and The Rudder as being April 4.

0516    *Spring—"Off to the country puffs the train" (Vesna— "Pomchal na dachu parovoz")* in The Rudder (Rul'). Berlin. May 10, 1925. pg. 2

0517    *Berlin Spring (Berlinskaya vesna)* in The Rudder (Rul'). Berlin. May 24, 1925. pg. 2

0518    *Exile (Izgnan'e)* in The Rudder (Rul'). Berlin. June 14, 1925. pg. 6

0519    *The Dream—"One night the window ledge" (Son— "Odnazhdy noch'yu podokonnik")* in The Rudder (Rul'). Berlin. June 30, 1925. pg. 2

0520    *Resurrection of the Dead (Voskresenie myortvykh)* in Renaissance (Vozrozhdenie). Paris. July 19, 1925

0521    *Paradise (Raj)* in The Rudder (Rul'). Berlin. July 26, 1925. pg. 2

0522   *The Train Accident (Krushenie)* in The Rudder (Rul'). Berlin. August 16, 1925. pg. 7; and in The Word (Slovo). Riga. No. 27. 1926

0523   *The Shadow (Ten')* in The Rudder (Rul'). Berlin. September 13, 1925. pg. 2

0524   *The Summit (Vershina)* in The Rudder (Rul'). Berlin. September 19, 1925. pg. 2
       Written August 31, 1925

0525   English: *I Like That Mountain.* Translated by Vladimir Nabokov in **Poems and Problems.** *0353*

0526   *The Path (Put')* in The Rudder (Rul'). Berlin. December 13, 1925. pg. 2

0527   *A Passer-by with a Christmas Tree (Prokhozhij s yolkoj)* in The Rudder (Rul'). Berlin. December 25, 1925. pg. 2

0528   *Shakespeare (Shekspir)* in The Fire-Bird (Zhar-Ptitsa). No. 12. Berlin. 1925. pg. 32

0529   *The Skijump (Lyzhnyj pryzhok)* in The Rudder (Rul'). Berlin. January 24, 1926. pg. 2

0530   *The Grand Piano (Royal')* in Gazette of the Ball of the Press (Gazeta Bala Pressy). No. 1. Berlin. February 14, 1926
       A special publication printed in connection with a benefit dance for needy Russian writers and journalists.

0531   *Soft Sound (Tikhij shum)* in The Rudder (Rul'). Berlin. April 10, 1926

Only an incomplete issue of The Rudder was available for examination, and hence this listing may be in error.

0532 English: *Soft Sound*. Translated by Vladimir Nabokov in **Poems and Problems.** *0353*

0533 *Ut pictura poesis* (To M. V. Dobuzhinsky [M. V. Dobuzhinskomu]) in The Rudder (Rul'). Berlin. April 25, 1926. pg. 2

0534 *"A trifle, the name of a mast, a plan"* (*"Pustyak, nazvan'e machty, plan"*) in The Link (Zveno). Paris. July 3–4, 1926
There is a minor misprint—a comma after *nazvan'e*—in the first line of this poem. The two sources for this poem give differing dates—July 3 and July 4—for its publication; the issue number of The Link in which it appears is No. 179.

0535 *The Room* (*Komnata*) in The Rudder (Rul'). Berlin. July 11, 1926. pg. 2

0536 *The Airplane—"How it sings, how unexpected"* (*Aèroplan— "Kak poyot on, kak nezhdanno"*) in The Rudder (Rul'). Berlin. July 25, 1926. pg. 2

0537 *Dreams* (*Sny*) in The Rudder (Rul'). Berlin. August 8, 1926. pg. 2

0538 *An Enchanting Season* (*Prelestnaya pora*) in The Rudder (Rul'). Berlin. October 17, 1926. pg. 2

0539 *Anniversary* (*Godovshchina*) in The Rudder (Rul'). Berlin. November 7, 1926. pg. 2

0540    *The Pilgrim (Palomnik)* in The Rudder (Rul'). Berlin. February 13, 1927. pg. 2

0541    *A Vision in a Dream (Snovidenie)* in The Rudder (Rul'). Berlin. May 1, 1927. pg. 2

0542    English: *The Dream.* Translated by Vladimir Nabokov in **Poems and Problems.** *0353*

0543    *Native Land—"Our happiness that is immortal" (Rodina— "Bessmertnoe schastie nashe").* Printed as a special edition in the form of a pamphlet sold for the benefit of a charity, June 4, 1927; and in The Rudder (Rul'). Berlin. June 15, 1927

0544    *The Ticket (Bilet)* in The Rudder (Rul'). Berlin. June 26, 1927. pg. 2

0545    *The Snapshot (Snimok)* in The Rudder (Rul'). Berlin. August 28, 1927. pg. 2
Written August 10, 1927

0546    English: *The Snapshot.* Translated by Vladimir Nabokov in **Poems and Problems.** *0353*

0547    *The Chess Knight (Shakhmatnyj kon')* in The Rudder (Rul'). Berlin. October 23, 1927. pg. 2

0548    *A University Poem (Universitetskaya poèma)* in Contemporary Annals (Sovremennye Zapiski). No. 33. Paris. 1927. pp. 223–254

0549    *The Execution (Rasstrel)* in The Rudder (Rul'). Berlin. January 8, 1928. pg. 2
Written in late 1927

0550      English: *The Execution*. Translated by Vladimir Nabokov in **Poems and Problems.** *0353*

0551      *The Cinema (Kinematograf)* in The Rudder (Rul'). Berlin. February 25, 1928. pg. 2

0552      *To My Soul (K dushe)* in The Rudder (Rul'). Berlin. March 18, 1928. pg. 2. Included under the title *In Paradise* in **The Return of Chorb.** *0279*
Written September 23, 1927

0553      English: *In Paradise*. Translated by A. Field in Nabokov—His Life in Art. Boston. Little, Brown. 1967

0554      *In Paradise*. Translated by Vladimir Nabokov in **Poems and Problems.** *0353*

0555      *The Islands (Ostrova)* in The Rudder (Rul'). Berlin. March 25, 1928. pg. 2

0556      *Bricks (Kirpichi)* in The Rudder (Rul'). Berlin. April 1, 1928. pg. 2

0557      *Conversation (Razgovor)* in The Rudder (Rul'). Berlin. April 14, 1928

0558      *Lilac (Siren')* in The Rudder (Rul'). Berlin. May 13, 1928. pg. 2

0559      *"For happiness the lover cannot sleep" ("Ot schastiya vlyublyonnomu ne spitsya")* in The Rudder (Rul'). Berlin. June 14, 1928
Written May 18, 1928

0560  English: *For Happiness the Lover Cannot Sleep.* Translated by Vladimir Nabokov in **Poems and Problems.** *0353*

0561  *The Wasp (Osa)* in The Rudder (Rul'). Berlin. June 24, 1928. pg. 2

0562  *To Russia—"My palm a strict geographer" (K Rossii— "Moyu ladon' geograf strogij")* in The Rudder (Rul'). Berlin. July 1, 1928. pg. 2

0563  *Tolstoy (Tolstoj)* in The Rudder (Rul'). Berlin. September 16, 1928. pg. 2

    Reprinted in Virgin Soil (Nov'). No. 8. Tallin. 1935. pp. 16–19

0564  *Stanzas on a Horse (Stansy o kone)* in The Rudder (Rul'). Berlin. February 2, 1929. pg. 2

0565  *"For traveling at night I do not need" ("Dlya stranstviya nochnogo mne ne nado")* in The Rudder (Rul'). Berlin. August 11, 1929. pg. 2

0566  *Aerial Island (Vozdushnyj ostrov)* in The Rudder (Rul'). Berlin. September 8, 1929. pg. 2

0567  *To the Muse (K muze)* in The Rudder (Rul'). Berlin. September 24, 1929. pg. 2
    Written September 14, 1929

    Reprinted in The Week (Nedelya). Paris. May 5, 1930?

0568  English: *The Muse.* Translated by Vladimir Nabokov in **Poems and Problems.** *0353*

0569       *Snow (Sneg); To an Unborn Reader (Nerodivshemusya chitatelyu)* in The Rudder (Rul'). Berlin. February 7, 1930. pg. 2

0570       English: *Snow.* Translated by Vladimir Nabokov in **Poems and Problems.** *0353*

0571       *First Love (Pervaya Lyubov')* in Russia and Slavdom (Rossiya i Slavyanstvo). Paris. April 19, 1930

           Reprinted in The Week (Nedelya). Paris. May 5, 1930?

0572       *Uldaborg: a translation from the Zoorlandian (Uldaborg: perevod s zoorlandskogo)* in The Rudder (Rul'). Berlin. May 4, 1930. pg. 2

0573       *The Presentation (Predstavlenie)* in Russia and Slavdom (Rossiya i Slavyanstvo). Paris. October 25, 1930

0574       *Poems (Stikhi)* in Russia and Slavdom (Rossiya i Slavyanstvo). No. 100. Paris. October ?, 1930

0575       *The Formula (Formula)* in The Rudder (Rul'). Berlin. April 5, 1931. pg. 2

0576       English: *The Formula.* Translated by Vladimir Nabokov in **Poems and Problems.** *0353*

0577       *From a Poem by Calmbrood (Iz Kalmbrudovoj poèmy)* in The Rudder (Rul'). Berlin. July 5, 1931. pg. 2
           A pretended translation of *The Night Journey* by the non-existent writer Vivian Calmbrood.

0578     *The Awakening (Probuzhdenie); To a Grapefruit (Pomlpimusu)* in Contemporary Annals (Sovremennye Zapiski). No. 47. Paris. 1931. pp. 232–233

0579     *Poem—"Inspiration, rosy sky" (Stikhi—"Vdokhnoven'e, rozovoe nebo")* in The Latest News (Poslednie Novosti). Paris. July 31, 1932. pg. 3
       Written Summer, 1932. Published under the title *Evening on a Vacant Lot (Vecher na pustyre)* in **Poems 1929–1951.** *0306*
       In **Poems and Problems,** the poem is dedicated, for the first time, to the memory of V. D. N. (Nabokov's father). *0353*

0580     English: *Evening on a Vacant Lot.* Translated by Vladimir Nabokov in **Poems and Problems.** *0353*

0581     Italy: *Sera in un terreno vago.* Translated by Alberto Pescetto in Poesie. *0307*

0582     *"He was triangular, two-winged, and legless" ("Sam treugol'nyj dvukrylyj, beznogij")* in The Latest News (Poslednie Novosti). Paris. August 8, 1932
       It is possible that the date given may be incorrect; the issue number of the newspaper is 4137.

0583     *The Madman (Bezumets)* in The Latest News (Poslednie Novosti). Paris. January 29, 1933
       Written in January, 1933

0584     English: *The Madman.* Translated by Vladimir Nabokov in **Poems and Problems.** *0353*

0585     *Poem—"Kind of green, kind of gray" (Stikhi—"Takoj zelyonyj, seryj")* in The Latest News (Poslednie Novosti). Paris. May 3, 1934. pg. 3

Published with the title *How I Love You* in **Poems 1929–1951.** *0306*

0586      English: *How I Love You.* Translated by Vladimir Nabokov in **Poems and Problems.** *0353*
First published in The New Yorker. New York. May 23, 1972

0587      Italy: *Como ti amo.* Translated by Alberto Pescetto in Poesie. *0307*

0588      *"Urging on the outcome of this life"* (*"Toropya ètoj zhizni razvyazku"*) in The Latest News (Poslednie Novosti). Paris. June 28, 1934. pg. 3; and The Projector (Prozhektor). Shanghai. August 4, 1934
The title was changed to *L'Inconnue de la Seine* in **Poems 1929–1951.** *0306*

0589      English: *L'Inconnue de la Seine.* Translated by Vladimir Nabokov in **Poems and Problems.** *0353*

0590      Italy: *L'inconnue de la Seine.* Translated by Alberto Pescetto in Poesie. *0307*

0590A      *The Poets* (*Poety*) in Contemporary Annals (Sovremennye Zapiski). No. 69. Paris. 1939. pp. 214–215

0591      *The Appeal*—*"Will you leave me alone, I implore you!"* (*Obrashchenie*—*"Otvyazhis' ya tebya umolyayu!"*) in Contemporary Annals (Sovremennye Zapiski). No. 70. Paris. 1940. pp. 128–129
This poem was signed with the pseudonym Vasilij Shishkov.

0592      English: *To Russia* (*"Will you leave me alone, I implore you!"*). Translated by Vladimir Nabokov in **Poems and**

Problems. *0353.* Also in **Poems (Stikhotvoreniya),**
**Poesie** and Tri-Quarterly. *0306, 0307*

0593    Italy: *Ti supplico—lasciami!* Translated by Alberto
Pescetto in Poesie. *0307*

0594    *The Softest of Tongues* in The Atlantic Monthly. Boston.
December 1941. pg. 765

0595    *A Literary Dinner* in The New Yorker. New York. April
11, 1942

    Reprinted in Songs and Dreams. Glasgow. Blackie &
Son Ltd. 1970

0596    Italy: *Un pranzo letterario.* Translated by Enzo Siciliano
in Poesie. *0307*

0597    *The Refrigerator Awakes* in The New Yorker. New York.
June 6, 1942. pg. 20

0598    Italy: *Il frigorifero si desta.* Translated by Enzo Siciliano
in Poesie. *0307*

0599    *Exile* in The New Yorker. New York. October 24, 1942. pg.
26

0600    *The Water Nymph—A Concluding Scene to Pushkin's*
Rusalka (*Rusalka—Zaklyuchitel'naya tsena k push-*
*kinskoj* Rusalke) in The New Review (Novyj Zhurnal). No.
2. New York. 1942. pp. 181–184
    A conclusion to Pushkin's unfinished dramatic poem.

0601    *Fame (Slava)* in The New Review (Novyj Zhurnal). No. 3.
New York. 1942. pp. 157–161

Written in 1942

0602     English: *Fame.* Translated by Vladimir Nabokov in **Poems and Problems.** *0353*

0603     Italy: *La gloria.* Translated by Alberto Pescetto in Poesie. *0307*

0604     *"When he was small"* in The Atlantic Monthly. Boston. January 1943. pg. 116

0605     *On Discovering a Butterfly* in The New Yorker. New York. May 15, 1943. pg. 26
This title was changed to *A Discovery* in **Poems** (*1959*). *0335*

0606     Italy: *Una scoperta.* Translated by Enzo Siciliano in Poesie. *0307*

0607     *"Not the sunset poem you make"* in The New Yorker. New York. June 10, 1944. pg. 30
Published under the title *The Poem* in **Poems.** *0335*

0608     Italy: *La poesia.* Translated by Enzo Siciliano in Poesie. *0307*

0609     *A Parisian Poem* (*Parizhskaya poèma*) in The New Review (Novyj Zhurnal). No. 7. New York. 1944. pp. 159–163
Written in 1943

0610     English: *The Paris Poem.* Translated by Vladimir Nabokov in **Poems and Problems.** *0353*

0611  Italy: *Poema di Parigi*. Translated by Alberto Pescetto in Poesie. *0307*

0612  *"No matter in what battle piece depicted"* (*"Kakim by polotnom batal'nym ni yavlyalas'"*) in The Socialist Messenger (Sotsialisticheskij Vestnik). New York. No. 37. 1944
This poem was published here for the first time anonymously and without the author's knowledge.

0613  English: *No Matter How*. Translated by Vladimir Nabokov in Modern Russian Poetry edited by V. Markov and M. Sparks. London. McGibbon & Kee. 1966

    Included in **Poems and Problems.** *0353*

0614  *An Evening of Russian Poetry* in The New Yorker. New York. March 3, 1945. pp. 23–24

0615  Italy: *Una serata di poesia russa*. Translated by Enzo Siciliano in Poesie. *0307*

0616  *On Rulers (O pravitelyakh)* in The New Review. (Novyj Zhurnal). No. 10. New York. 1945. pp. 172–173
Written in 1944

0617  English: *On Rulers*. Translated by Vladimir Nabokov in **Poems and Problems.** *0353*

0618  Italy: *Sui governanti*. Translated by Alberto Pescetto in Poesie. *0307*

0619  *Dream* in The Atlantic Monthly. Boston. September 1946. pg. 63

0620 *To Prince S. M. Kachurin* (*Kn. S. M. Kachurinu*) in The New Review (Novyj Zhurnal). No. 15. New York. 1947. pp. 81–83
  Written in early 1947

  Included in Èstafeta edited by I. Yassen, V. Andreev, and Yu. Terapiano. Paris. New York. Maison du Livre Étranger. 1948

0621 English: *To Prince S. M. Kachurin.* Translated by Vladimir Nabokov in **Poems and Problems.** *0353*
  In this printing the poem has the subtitle *An Epistle in Verse* (*Poslanie v stikhakh*) which it lacked in its initial appearance.

0622 Italy: *Al principe S. M. Kacurin.* Translated by Alberto Pescetto in Poesie. *0307*

0623 *The Room* in The New Yorker. New York. January 27, 1951. pg. 34

0624 Italy: *La stanza.* Translated by Enzo Siciliano in Poesie. *0307*

0625 *Voluptates tactionum* in The New Yorker. New York. January 27, 1951. pg. 30

0626 Italy: *Voluptates tactionum.* Translated by Enzo Siciliano in Poesie. *0307*

0627 *Lines Written in Oregon* in The New Yorker. New York. August 29, 1953. pg. 28

0628 Italy: *Versi scritti nell'Oregon.* Translated by Enzo Siciliano in Poesie. *0307*

0629    *Irregular Iambics* (*Nepravil'nye yamby*) in Essays (Opyty). No. 1. New York. 1953. pg. 41

0630    English: *Irregular Iambics.* Translated by Vladimir Nabokov in **Poems and Problems.** *0353*
This reprinting corrects a misprint in the original publication.

0631    *On Translating* "Eugene Onegin" in The New Yorker. New York. January 8, 1955. pg. 34

0632    Italy: *Nel tradurre* "Eugenio Onieghin." Translated by Enzo Siciliano in Poesie. *0307*

0633    *Ode to a Model* in The New Yorker. New York. October 8, 1955. pg. 48

0634    Italy: *Ode a una modella.* Translated by Enzo Siciliano in Poesie. *0307*

0635    *Rain* in The New Yorker. New York. April 21, 1956. pg. 43

0636    Italy: *Pioggia.* Translated by Enzo Siciliano in Poesie. *0307*

0637    *Seven Poems* (*Sem' stikhotvorenij*): "As over verse of medium power" ("Kak nad stikhami sily srednej"); "Into the high-ceilinged studio there fully" ("Tselikom v masterskuyu vysokuyu"); "All that constrains the heart" ("Vsyo, ot chego ono szhimaetsya"); "The evening is hazy and long" ("Vecher dymchat i dolog"); "Whatever happiness or grief" ("Kakoe b schast'e ili gore"); "There is this dream, repeating like the languid" ("Est' son. On povtoryaetsya, kak tomnyj"); "Could the gray winters have washed away" ("Zimy li serye smyli") in The New Review (Novyj Zhurnal). No. 46. New York. 1956. pp. 43–46

A poem-cycle written in 1953. In the printing of this cycle the last two strophes of *"All that constrains the heart"* have been cut off by mistake and set as a separate poem.

0638    *Ballad of Longwood Glen* in The New Yorker. New York. July 6, 1957. pg. 27

0639    Italy: *La ballata della valletta di Longwood*. Translated by Enzo Siciliano in Poesie.  *0307*

0640    *Two Poems (Dva stikhotvoreniya): "What is the evil deed I have committed?"* (*"Kakoe sdelal ya durnoe delo?"*); *"There are such moments: 'it can't be,' you mutter"* (*"Minuty est': 'Ne mozhet byt,' bormochesh"*) in Aerial Ways (Vozdushnye Puti). No. 2. New York. 1961. pp. 184–185
Written December 27, 1959

0641    English: *"What is the evil deed I have committed?"* in Newsweek. New York. June 25, 1962

0642    *"What is the Evil Deed."* Translated by Vladimir Nabokov in Modern Russian Poetry edited by V. Markov and M. Sparks. London. McGibbon & Kee. 1966. Included in **Poems and Problems.**  *0353*

0643    Germany: "Lolita." Translated by Zavier Schaffgotsch in Frankfurter Allgemeine Zeitung. Frankfurt. January 18, 1964
An unauthorized translation of *"What is the evil deed I have committed?"*

0644    *Lunar Lines* in The New York Review of Books. New York. April 28, 1966

0645    *"Forty-three or four years"* (*"Sorok tri ili chetyre goda"*) in Aerial Ways (Vozdushnye Puti). No. 5. New York. 1967. pg. 84
    Written April 9, 1967

0646    *"From the gray north"* (*"S serogo severa"*) in The New Russian Word (Novoe Russkoe Slovo). New York. January 21, 1968
    This poem was published as a holograph photo. Written December 20, 1967

0647    English: *From the Gray North.* Translated by Vladimir Nabokov in **Poems and Problems.** *0353*

0648    *The Poets—"Hallward, out of the room a candle passes"* (*"Poèty—"Iz komnaty v seni svecha perekhodit"*) in Tri-Quarterly. No. 17. Illinois. Winter, 1970. pp. 4–5
    Printed with facing Russian text.

0649    *The Cossack* (*Kazak*) in Tri-Quarterly. No. 17. Winter, 1970. pg. 218
    This poem, which may be read from left to right and right to left, appears as a holograph photo, together with an English version by I. Weil; the poem was written in February 1939, but never before appeared in print. In Supplement to Tri-Quarterly No. 17—see *0650*—Nabokov points out errors in the Weil translation.

0650    *"The querulous gawk of"* in Supplement to Tri-Quarterly. No. 17. Illinois. 1970. pg. 15

# Novels and
# Short Story
# Collections

0651   **MARY (MASHEN'KA).** Berlin. Slovo. 1926. 196pp. Novel

Excerpt in The Word (Slovo). No. 111. Riga. March 27–28, 1926

0652   English: **Mary.** Translated by Michael Glenny and Vladimir Nabokov. New York. McGraw-Hill. 1970; and London. Weidenfeld & Nicolson. 1971.

0653   Germany: **Sie kommt—kommt sie?** Translated by J. M. Schubert and Gregor Jarcho. Berlin. Ullstein. 1928

Serialized under the title **Maschenjka kommt** in Vossische Zeitung. Nos. 154–167. Berlin. July 1928

0654   Italy: **Maria.** Translated by Ettore Capriolo. Milan. Mondadori. 1971

0655   The Netherlands: **Masjenka.** Translated by J. F. Kliphuis. Amsterdam. H. Meulenhoff. 1971

0655A   Spain: **Mashenka.** Translated by Andres Bosch. Barcelona. Editorial Lumen. 1972

0656   **KING, QUEEN, KNAVE (KOROL', DAMA, VALET).** Berlin. Slovo. 1928. 260pp. Novel

Excerpt in The Rudder (Rul'). Berlin. September 23, 1928. pp. 2–3

New Russian edition with Foreword. New York. McGraw-Hill. 1969

0657   English: **King, Queen, Knave.** Translated by Dmitri Nabokov and Vladimir Nabokov. New York. McGraw-Hill. 1968; and London. Weidenfeld & Nicolson. 1968. 272pp.

The first American edition (April 1968) was defective and was destroyed except for a few copies;

the first regular edition was published in May 1968 and a Book-of-the-Month Club edition appeared in June 1968.

Reprinted: New York. Crest. 1969

Reprinted: London. Panther. 1970

Adapted as a film by Wolper Productions
This film had not yet been released as this manuscript closed.

0658    Argentina: **Rei, Valete & Dama**. Translated by Luiz Corção. Rio de Janeiro. O Cruzeiro. 1969

0659    Czechoslovakia: Excerpts from **Král, dáma, kluk**. Translated by A. Isačenko in Annals of Literature and Criticism (Listy pro umeni a kritiku). Nos. 13–14. Prague. 1934

0660    Finland: **Kuningas, Rouva, Sotamies**. Translated by Juhani Jaskari. Jyväskylä. K. J. Gummerus. 1969

0661    France: **Roi, Dame, Valet**. Translated by Georges Magnane. Gallimard. Paris. 1971

0662    Germany: **König, Dame, Bube. Ein Spiel mit dem Schicksal**. Translated by Siegfried von Vegesack. Berlin. Ullstein. 1930

Serialized in Vossische Zeitung. March 15–April 17, 1930

Reprinted: Reinbek. Rowohlt. 1959, 1961, 1962; special edition by the Bertelsmann Lesering. 1960

0663    The Netherlands: **Heer, Vrouw, Boer**. Translated by J. W. Staalman. Utrecht. Bruna & Zoon. 1963

*0664*    **Heer, Vrouw, Boer.** Translated by M. and L. Coutinho.
Amsterdam. De Bezige Bij. 1970

*0664A*    **Konge, Dame, Knaegt.** Translated by Mogens Boisen.
Amsterdam. H. Meulenhoff. 1971

*0665*    Sweden: **Kung, Dam, Knekt.** Translated by Estrid
Tenggren. Stockholm. Alb Bonniers. 1969, 1971

*0666*  **THE DEFENSE (ZASHCHITA LUZHINA).** Berlin. Slovo. 1930.
234pp. Novel

Serialized in Contemporary Annals (Sovremennye Zapiski).
Nos. 40–42. Paris. 1929–30

Excerpts in The Rudder (Rul'). Berlin. September 15, 1929
and January 12, 1930

Reprinted: Paris. Éditions de la Seine. 1967

*0667*    English: **The Defense.** Translated by Michael Scammell
and Vladimir Nabokov. New York. G. P. Putnam's
Sons. 1964; and London. Weidenfeld & Nicolson. 1964.
256pp.

Serialized in The New Yorker. New York. May 9 and
16, 1964

Reprinted: New York. Popular Library. 1965

Reprinted: London. Panther. 1967

Reprinted: New York. Capricorn. 1970

*0668*    Denmark: **Forsvaret.** Translated by Morten Piil. Copenhagen. Gyldendal. 1968.

*0669*    Finland: **Luzinin Puolustus.** Translated by Juhani Jaskari.
Jyväskylä. K. J. Gummerus. 1966

0670    France: **La course du fou.** Translated by Denis Roche. Paris. Fayard. 1934

0671    **La Défense Loujine.** Translated by Genia and René Cannac. Paris. Gallimard. 1964

0672    Germany: **Lushins Verteidigung.** Translated by Dietmar Schulte. Reinbek. Rowohlt. 1961

   Excerpt entitled "Die unterbrochene Partie" in Das Schoenste. Volume 7. No. 10. Munich. October 1961

   Excerpt in Hannoversche Rundschau. Hanover. October 26, 1961

   Reprinted: Frankfurt, Vienna, Zurich. Büchergilde Gutenberg. 1965

0673    Italy: **La Difesa.** Translated by Bruno Oddera. Milan. Mondadori. 1968

0674    Mexico: **La Defensa.** Translated by Carlos Barrera. Mexico. Diana. 1965

0675    The Netherlands: **De verdediging.** Translated by M. and L. Coutinho. Amsterdam. De Bezige Bij. 1967

0676    Norway: **Forsvaret.** Oslo. Cappelens Förlag. 1970

0677    Sweden: **Han som spelade schack med livet.** Translated by Ellen Rydelius. Stockholm. Bonniers. 1936, 1966
   In the 1966 edition the translation was revised by Harriet Alfons.

0678    **THE RETURN OF CHORB: Stories and Poems (VOZVRASHCHENIE CHORBA: Rasskazy i Stikhi).** Berlin. Slovo. 1930. 246pp. Short stories

See also poems listing.  *0279*

*0693*    *Terror (Uzhas)*                                             *0929*

*0694*  **THE EYE (SOGLYADATAJ)** in Contemporary Annals
(Sovremennye Zapiski). No. 44. Paris. 1930. pp. 91–152; and
an excerpt in The Latest News (Poslednie Novosti). Paris.
October 12, 1930. pp. 2–3. Novel
See also **The Eye** as the title novella of the 1938 short
story collection. *0743*

*0695*        English: **The Eye.** Translated by Dmitri Nabokov and
Vladimir Nabokov. New York. Phaedra. 1965; and
London. Weidenfeld & Nicolson. 1966

Serialized in Playboy. Chicago. January–March 1965

Reprinted: New York. Pocket Books. 1967

Reprinted: London. Panther. 1968

*0696*        Brazil: **O Ôlho Vigilante.** Translated by Heitor P. Froes.
Rio de Janeiro. Jose Olympio. 1967

*0697*        Finland: **Silma.** Translated by Juhani Jaskari. Jyväskylä.
K. G. Gummerus. 1968

*0698*        France: **L'Aguet.** Translated by Denis Roche in Les
Oeuvres Libres. No. 164. Paris. 1935

*0699*        **Le Guetteur.** Translated by Georges Magnane. Paris.
Gallimard. 1968

*0700*        Italy: **L'Occhio.** Translated by Bruno Oddera. Milan.
Mondadori. 1967

*0701*        Japan: **Me.** Translated by Toyoki Ogasawara. Tokyo.
Hakusuisha. 1967

Published together with **Nabokov's Quartet** through arrangements with Orion Press.

0702    The Netherlands: **Het Oog.** Translated by M. Coutinho. Amsterdam. De Bezige Bij. 1966

0703    Spain: **El Ojo.** Translated by Mireia Bofill. Barcelona. Ediciones Martinez Roca. 1967

0704    **CAMERA OBSCURA (KAMERA OBSKURA).** Paris. Contemporary Annals Publishing House (Izdatel'stvo Sovremennye Zapiski). 1932. 204pp. Novel

Excerpts in The Latest News (Poslednie Novosti). Paris. April 17 and September 18, 1932

Excerpt "Darkness" ("T'ma") in Our Age (Nash Vek). Berlin. November 8, 1931. pg. 2

Serialized in Contemporary Annals (Sovremennye Zapiski). Nos. 49–52. Paris. 1932–33

Reprinted: Berlin. Parabola-Petropolis. 1933

0705    English: **Camera obscura.** Translated by W. Roy. London. John Long. 1936

0706    **Laughter in the Dark.** Translated by Vladimir Nabokov. Indianapolis/New York. The Bobbs-Merrill Co. 1938. 292pp

Reprinted: New York. New American Library. 1950

Reprinted: New York. Berkeley Press. 1958, 1961

Reprinted: New York. New Directions. 1960

Reprinted: London. Weidenfeld & Nicolson. 1961

Reprinted: Harmondsworth. Penguin Books. 1961, 1963, 1969

Adapted as a film. Directed by Tony Richardson. A Woodfall Film. 1968

0707      Brazil: **Gargalhada na escuridão.** Translated by Brenno Silveira. São Paulo. Boa Leitura. 1961

0708      Czechoslovakia: Serialized in Česke Slovo. Prague. 1935. Queries in Czechoslovakia have failed to produce the precise date of this serialization.

0709      Denmark: **Latter i mørket.** Translated from the English by Henrik Larsen. Copenhagen. Hans Reitzel. 1960

     Reprinted: Copenhagen. Gyldendal. 1967

0710      Finland: **Naurua pimeässä.** Translated by Eila Pennanen and Juhani Jaskari. Jyväskylä. K. J. Gummerus. 1962, 1970

0711      France: **Chambre obscure.** Translated by Doussia Ergaz. Paris. Grasset. 1934, 1959

0712      Germany: **Gelächter im Dunkel.** Translated by Renate Gerhardt and Hans-Heinrich Wellmann. Reinbek. Rowohlt. 1962 (two editions plus a special edition for the Bertelsmann Lesering).

     Serialized in Welt am Sontag. Hamburg. November 29, 1959–April 17, 1960

0713      Greece: **The Dark Blind-Alley (To skotina adiexodo).** Translated by Are Diktaios. Athens. Ekdoseis Phexes. 1960 An unauthorized translation.

0714      Italy: **Camera oscura.** Translated by Alessandra Iljina. Milan. Muggiani. 1947

0715      **Risata nel Buio.** Translated by Anna Malvezzi. Milan. Mondadori. 1961, 1963, 1969

0716      Japan: **Magda (Maguda)** by V. Nabokofu. Translated by Takoichi Kawasaki. Tokyo. Kawade shobo shina. 1960

0717      **Margot (Marugo).** Translated by Shinoda Hajime. Tokyo. Kawade shobo shina. 1967.
An unauthorized translation.

0718      Mexico: **Risa en la oscuridad.** Translated by Betty Castellanos. Mexico City. Axteca. 1959
An unauthorized translation.

0719      The Netherlands: **Lach in het donker.** Translated by M. Coutinho. The Hague. Oisterwijk. 1960

0720      Spain: **Camera obscura.** Translated by Jose Maria Riba Ricart. Barcelona. Luis de Caralt. 1951

0721      **Risa en la oscuridad.** Translated by Antonio Samons. Barcelona. Plaza & Janes. 1961, 1969

0722      Sweden: **Camera obscura.** Translated by Hjalmar Dahl. Helsingfors. Holger Schildts. 1935

0723      **Skratt i mörkret.** Translated by Caj Lundgren. Stockholm. Wahlstrom & Widstrand. 1969

0724      United Arab Republic: **Laughter in the Dark (Dahikā-tun fil-zalām).** Translated by Zaki Shimudah. Cairo. Hilmi Murad. 1961
An unauthorized translation.

0725  **THE EXPLOIT (PODVIG).** Paris. Contemporary Annals Publishing House (Izdatel'stvo Sovremennye Zapiski). 1933. 235pp. Novel

Excerpts in The Latest News (Poslednie Novosti). Paris. January 14 and April 12, 1931

Excerpts entitled "Excerpt from the Novel Podvig" and "Zoorlandia" (the third excerpt only) in Russia and Slavdom (Rossiya i Slavyanstvo). Paris. January 17, April 25, and October 3, 1931

Serialized in Contemporary Annals (Sovremennye Zapiski). Nos. 45–48. Paris. 1931–32

0726    English: **Glory.** Translated by Dmitri Nabokov and Vladimir Nabokov. New York. McGraw-Hill. 1972; and London. Weidenfeld & Nicolson. 1972

Excerpt entitled "A Russian at Cambridge" in The London Times. London. March 11, 1972

0727    **DESPAIR (OTCHAYANIE).** Berlin. Petropolis. 1936. Novel

Excerpts in The Latest News (Poslednie Novosti). Paris: *Despair (Otchayanie).* December 31, 1932. *Still ist die Nacht.* October 8, 1933. *Ardalion's Departure (Ot'ezd Ardaliona).* November 5, 1933

Serialized in Contemporary Annals (Sovremennye Zapiski). Nos. 54–56. Paris. 1934. pp. 108–161; 70–116

0728    English: **Despair.** Translated by Vladimir Nabokov. London. John Long. 1937

Serialized in Playboy. Chicago. December–February 1965–66
In its second English translation which first appeared in Playboy the text of the novel has many revisions and additions.

Reprinted: New York. G. P. Putnam's Sons. 1966; and London. Weidenfeld & Nicolson. 1966. 222pp

Reprinted: New York. Pocket Books. 1966

Reprinted: London. Panther. 1969

Reprinted: New York. Capricorn. 1970

See also Nabokov's Congeries. *1242*

*0729*   Denmark: **Fortvivlelse.** Translated from the English by Morten Piil. Copenhagen. Gyldendal. 1967

*0730*   France: **La méprise.** Translated from the English by Marcel Stora. Paris. Gallimard. 1939, 1959

*0731*   Japan: **Zetsubo.** Translated by Otsu Eiichirô. Tokyo. Hakusuisha. 1969

*0732*   Spain: **El engaño.** Translated by Fernando Gutierrez. Barcelona. Mateu-F.I.C.S.A. 1960
In this edition Nabokov's Christian name is spelled Wladimir.

*0733*   **Desesperacion.** Translated by Ramon Margalef. Barcelona. Luis de Caralt. 1969

*0734*   **THE GIFT (DAR)** in Contemporary Annals (Sovremennye Zapiski). Nos. 63–67. Paris. 1937–38. Novel
Chapter 4 was not included in this publication.

Excerpt entitled "The Present" ("Podarok") in The Latest News (Poslednie Novosti). Paris. March 28, 1937

Excerpt entitled "The Return" ("Vozvrashchenie") in The Latest News (Poslednie Novosti). Paris. December 25, 1937

Excerpt entitled "A Stroll in the Grunewald" ("Progulka v Gruneval'de") in The Latest News (Poslednie Novosti). Paris. February 15, 1938

Reprinted: New York. Chekhov Publishing House (Izdatel'stvo imeni Chekhova). 1952. 411pp.
The first publication in book-form and in its entirety. It is dedicated to the memory of the author's mother.

0735      English: **The Gift.** Translated by Michael Scammell, Dmitri Nabokov, and Vladimir Nabokov. New York. G. P. Putnam's Sons. 1963; and London. Weidenfeld & Nicolson. 1963. 378pp.
See also Nabokov's Congeries. *1242*

Excerpt entitled "Triangle in a Circle" in The New Yorker. New York. March 23, 1963

Excerpt entitled "The Lyre" in The New Yorker. New York. April 13, 1963

Reprinted: New York. Berkeley. Popular Library. 1963

Reprinted: London. Panther. 1966
With a cover by the author's son, Dmitri Nabokov

Reprinted: New York. Capricorn. 1970

0736      Denmark: **Gaven.** Translated by Else and Jørgen Andersen. Copenhagen. Gyldendal. 1966, 1967
The 1966 edition was defective and was destroyed.

0737      Finland: **Lahja.** Translated by Juhani Jaskari. Jyväskylä. K. J. Gummerus. 1965

0738      France: **Le Don.** Translated by Raymond Girard. Paris. Gallimard-Du Monde Entier. 1967

Excerpt entitled "Toutes les horloges de la maison." Translated by Raymond Girard in La Revue de Paris. Paris. November 1967

0739      Italy: **Il Dono.** Translated by Bruno Oddera. Milan. Mondadori. 1966

Excerpts entitled "Triangolo nel cerchil." Translated by Bruno Oddera in Panorama. No. 14. Milan. November 1963

0740      Japan: **Shibutsu.** Translated by Otsu Eüchiro. Tokyo. Hakusuisha. 1965

0741      Mexico: **El Don.** Translated by Carlos Barrera. Mexico. Diana. 1965

0742      Sweden: **Gavan.** Translated by Filippa Rolf. Stockholm. Bonniers. 1965

0743      **THE EYE (SOGLYADATAJ).** Paris. Russian Annals Publishing House (Izdatel'stvo Russkie Zapiski). 1938. 252pp. A short novel and twelve short stories

0744      The Eye (Soglyadataj)           0694
          See **The Eye** as a novel.

0745      The Offense (Obida)           0943

0746      Goosefoot (Lebeda)           0750

0747      Terra incognita           0945

0748      The Meeting (Vstrecha)           0947

0749      A Dashing Fellow (Khvat)           0972

0750      The Busy Man (Zanyatoj chelovek)           0944

0751      Music (Muzyka)           0951

0752      Pilgram (Pil'gram)           0936

0753      Perfection (Sovershenstvo)           0956

0754   *The Beauty (Krasavitsa)*                                     *0965*


0755   *An Event from Life (Sluchaj iz zhizni)*                      *0978*


0756   *Breaking the News (Opoveshchenie)*


0757   Germany: **Die Benachrichtigung.** Translated by W. Jollos
       in Neue Zürcher Zeitung. Nos. 817, 818. Zurich. May 12,
       13, 1936.
       The original Russian publication from which this
       translation was evidently made has not been located.


0758   **INVITATION TO A BEHEADING (PRIGLASHENIE NA KAZN').**
       Paris. Dom Knigi. 1938. 205pp. Novel

       Serialized in Contemporary Annals (Sovremennye Zapiski).
       Nos. 58–60. Paris. 1935–36

       Reprinted: Berlin. Dom Knigi. 1938

       Reprinted: Paris. Éditions Victor. 1966
       A private edition.


0759   English: **Invitation to a Beheading.** Translated by Dmitri
       Nabokov and Vladimir Nabokov. New York. G. P.
       Putnam's Sons. 1959; and London. Weidenfeld &
       Nicolson. 1960. 208pp.
       See also Nabokov's Congeries.  *1242*

       Reprinted: Greenwich, Connecticut. Fawcett Publica-
       tions. 1960, 1965

       Reprinted: Harmondsworth. Penguin Books. 1962,
       1963, 1969

       Reprinted: New York. Capricorn Books. 1965

       Reprinted: London. Panther. 1969

       Adapted for the stage by Russell McGrath, produced
       by J. Papp in the New York Shakespeare Festival.
       1969

0760    Argentina: **Invitado a una decapitación** in Sur. Buenos Aires. n.d.
An unauthorized translation.

0761    Denmark: **Invitation til skafottet.** Translated from the English by Jørgen Andersen. Copenhagen. Gyldendal. 1962

Adapted as a Danish television opera. Music by Ib Nørholm, libretto by Paul Borum. 1967

0762    France: **Invitation au supplice.** Translated by Jarl Priel. Paris. Gallimard. 1960

0763    Germany: **Invitation to a Beheading.** Translated by Dieter E. Zimmer. Reinbek. Rowohlt. 1970
The title of this translation was not received as this manuscript closed.

0764    Italy: **Invito a una decapitazione.** Translated by Bruno Oddera. Milan. Mondadori. 1961

0765    The Netherlands: **Uitnodiging voor een Onthoofding.** Translated by M. and L. Coutinho. Amsterdam. De Bezige Bij. 1970

0766    Norway: **Date with the Executioner (Stevnemøte med bøddelen).** Translated from the English by Colbjørn Helander. Oslo. Cappelen. 1961

0767    United Arab Republic: **Wolves' Banquet (Ma'dabat Al-dhi'āb).** Translated by Muhammad Tawfiq Mustafa al-Quhirah: Dar al-Datib al-Arabi. n.d.
An unauthorized translation.

*0768*  **SOLUS REX** in Contemporary Annals (Sovremennye Zapiski). No. 70. Paris. 1940. pp. 5–36. A second portion entitled *Ultima Thule* appeared in The New Review (Novyj Zhurnal). No. 1. New York. 1942. *0841* Unfinished novel
Both of these portions of the novel have been translated in the collection **A Russian Beauty.** *0891*

*0769*  **THE REAL LIFE OF SEBASTIAN KNIGHT.** Norfolk, Connecticut. New Directions. 1941, 1959. 205pp. Novel

Reprinted: London. Poetry. 1945

Excerpt in The Psychology of Personal Constructs by George A. Kelly. New York. Norton. 1955

Excerpt in The Meaning of Fiction by Albert Cook. Detroit. Wayne State Press. 1960

Reprinted: London. Weidenfeld & Nicolson. 1960

Reprinted: Harmondsworth. Penguin Books. 1964, 1971

Excerpt in Practical Rhetoric by O. B. Hardison, Jr. New York. Appleton-Century-Crofts. 1966

*0770*  Argentina: **La verdadera vida de Sebastian Knight.** Translated by Enrique Pezzoni. Buenos Aires. Sur. 1959

*0771*  Austria: See Germany. *0775*

*0772*  Brazil: **A verdadeira vida de Sebastião Knight.** Translated by Brenno Silveira. Rio de Janeiro. Civilizacão Brasileira. 1961

*0773*  Finland: **Sebastian Knightin todellinen elämä.** Translated by Eila Pennanen and Juhani Jaskari. Jyväskylä. K. J. Gummerus. 1960

*0774*  France: **La vraie vie de Sebastian Knight.** Translated by Yvonne Davet. Paris. Albin Michel. 1951

Gallimard took over rights to this novel from Albin Michel but agreement with New Directions could not be reached because of demands unacceptable to the author. The 1962 Gallimard edition was withdrawn after selling a few hundred copies.

Excerpt in Mercure de France. Paris. August 1951

0775    Germany: **Das wahre Leben des Sebastian Knight.** Translated by Dieter E. Zimmer. Reinbek. Rowohlt. 1960

Reprinted: Berlin, Darmstadt, Vienna. Deutsche Buchgemeinschaft. 1970

0776    India: **A Real Life (Prajāpati jivan).** Translated by Devavrata Ray. Calcutta. Allahabad Rupa & Company. 1969
In Bengali.

0777    Italy: **La vera vita di Sebastiano Knight.** Translated by G. Fletzer. Milan. Bompiani. 1948.

0778    Japan: **Sebasuchan Nuito no sinzitu no syôgai.** Translated by Yosiyuki Fujikawa. Tokyo. Kodausha. 1970

0779    **BEND SINISTER.** New York. Henry Holt. 1947. 242pp. Novel

Reprinted: London. Weidenfeld & Nicolson. 1960

Reprinted: London. Transworld Publishers: Corgi Books. 1962

Reprinted: New York. Time Inc. Reading Program Special Edition. 1964
With a new introduction by the author.

Excerpt in The Sciences and Humanities edited by W. T. Jones. Berkeley. University of California Press. 1965

Reprinted: New York. McGraw-Hill. 1973

0780    Germany: **Das Bastardzeichen.** Translated by Dieter E. Zimmer. Reinbek. Rowohlt. 1962

0781    Italy: **I Bastardi.** Translated by Bruno Oddera. Milan. Rizzoli. 1967

0782    The Netherlands: **Bastaards.** Translated by Charles B. Timmer. Amsterdam. Van Oorschot. 1961, 1969

        Excerpt entitled "Gesprek over Hamlet." Translated by Charles B. Timmer in Libertinage. Amsterdam. September–October 1949

0783    **NINE STORIES.** Norfolk, Connecticut. New Directions. 1947 Short story collection.

0784    *The Aurelian*
        A translation of *Pil'gram* from the Russian collection     *0936*
        **The Eye.**

0785    *Cloud, Castle, Lake*                                              *0987*

0786    *Spring in Fialta*                                                *0979*

0787    *Mademoiselle O*                                                  *1009*

0788    *A Forgotten Poet*                                                *1027*

0789    *The Assistant Producer*                                          *1017*

0790    *'That in Aleppo Once. . .'*                                      *1022*

0791    *Time and Ebb*                                                    *1031*

0793    **LOLITA.** Paris. Olympia Press. 1955, 1958, 1959, 1960, 1961.
        Novel
        The 1955 edition was in two volumes (Vol. I, 190pp.; Vol.
        II, 223pp.) with an unsigned publisher's foreword. The
        1960 edition was one of The Traveller's Companion se-
        ries. Olympia Press also published L'affaire Lolita (See
        *0802*), a record of the book's early publishing history. See
        also the screenplay version of Lolita. *1076*

        Excerpt in Anchor Review. No. 2. New York. June 1957
        The excerpt appeared with significant omissions.

        Reprinted: New York. G. P. Putnam's Sons. 1958. 319pp.

        Reprinted: Israel. Steimatzky. n.d.

0794    Russian: **Lolita.** Translated by Vladimir Nabokov. New
        York. Phaedra. 1967 (two editions)
        With an introduction by the author: *Postscript to
        the Russian Edition (Postskriptum k russkomu
        izdaniyu)*. It should be noted that the "introduction"
        to **Lolita** is by a fictional character while the "real"
        introduction by Nabokov is appended to this novel
        as a Postscript.

0795    Argentina: **Lolita.** Translated by Enrique Tejedor.
        Buenos Aires. Sur. 1959

0796    Austria: see Germany. *0803*

0797    Brazil: **Lolita.** Translated by Brenno Silveira. Rio de
        Janeiro. Civilizacão Brasileira. 1959, 1970

        Reprinted: São Paulo. Boa Leitura. 1962

        Reprinted: Rio de Janeiro. Biblioteca Universal Popu-
        lar. 1968

0798     Denmark: **Lolita**. Translated by Tom Bright. Copenhagen. Hans Reitzel. 1957

0799     **Lolita**. Translated by Mogens Boisen. Copenhagen. Gyldendal. 1963, 1966, 1967, 1969

0800     Finland: **Lolita**. Translated by Eila Pennanen and Juhani Jaskari. Jyväskylä. Kompassi Pocket Book Series. K. J. Gummerus. 1959, 1963, 1969

0801     Formosa: **Lo li t'ai**. Translated by Chao Erh Hsin in Kuang Kuan Magazine. No. 170. Nan Kang. 1960
    An unauthorized translation.

0802     France: **Lolita**. Translated by Eric Kahane. Paris. Gallimard. 1959 (two editions)

Excerpt (Chapters 1–6 of Part I) in L'Affaire Lolita. Paris. Olympia Press. 1957. pp. 25–42
N.B. In this volume there is a translation by Eric Kahane ("Apropos de Lolita," pp. 43–50) of Nabokov's English Afterword to the novel. It was the first appearance of this essay in any language.

Reprinted: Paris. Livre de Poche. 1963

Excerpt entitled "Le Voyage de Lolita." Translated by Eric Kahane in La Nouvelle Revue Française. Paris. March 1, 1959

Excerpt in Les Lettres Nouvelles. No. 46. Paris. February, 1957

Excerpt in Les Chefs d'Oeuvres de l'Érotisme. Paris. Planète. 1965. 3pp.

Reprinted: Lausanne. La Guilde du Livre bookclub. 1966

0803     Germany: **Lolita**. Translated by Helen Hessel, Maria Carlsson, Kurt Kusenberg, K. M. Ledig-Rowohlt, and Gregor von Rezzori. Hamburg. Rowohlt. 1959, 1961, 1969

Reprinted: Reinbek. Rowohlt. 1962, 1964, 1965

Reprinted: Berlin, Darmstadt, Vienna. Deutsche Buchgemeinschatt. 1964

Reprinted: Stuttgart. Güterlohn Book Club. 1968

0804    Greece: **Lolita**. Translated by Andreas Pagualos. Athens. Gerolymbos. 1961
An unauthorized edition with an introduction by N. G. Stafatos.

Reprinted: Athens. Minotavros Philological Library. 1961 (two editions)
An unauthorized edition.

Reprinted: Athens. Dorikos Philological Library. n.d.

0805    India: **Lolitā**. Translated by Dhruvajyati Rāychaudhuri. Calcutta. Nāvik Prakasani. n.d.
In Bengali.

0806    **Laulitā**. Translated by Ararinda Nāth. Delhi. Anupama Pocket Books. 1967
In Hindi.

0807    Israel: **Lolita**. Translated into Hebrew by Edna Kornfeld and Yosef Warhaftig. Tel Aviv. Ankor. 1959, 1960

0808    **Lolita**. Translated into Polish in Survey (Przegład). Tel Aviv. No. 513. December 3, 1958—No. 549. August 12, 1959

The translator is not named.

0809    **Lolita**. Translated into Arabic by Fouad Daniel. Nazareth. Maronon el Agabri. 1962
An unauthorized translation.

0810      Italy: **Lolita**. Translated by Bruno Oddera. Milan. Mondadori. 1959–1963, 1966, 1970

0811      Japan: **Rorita**. Translated by Yasuo Ôkubo. Tokyo. Kawade shobô Shinsha. 1959, 1962. Two volumes

0812      The Lebanon: **Lolita**. Translated by Marwan Al Gabri. Beirut. The United Publishing House. 1959 (two editions)

0813      Mexico: **Lolita**. Mexico City. Azteca. 1959
         An unauthorized translation.

0814      **Lolita**. Translated by Enrique Tejador. Mexico City. Grijalbo. 1970

0815      The Netherlands: **Lolita**. Translated by M. Coutinho. The Hague. Oisterwijk. 1960

0816      Norway: **Lolita**. Translated by Odd Bang-Hansen. Oslo. Cappelens. 1959, 1969

0817      Poland: see Israel. *0807*

0818      Sweden: **Lolita**. Translated by Nils Kjellström. Stockholm. Wahlström & Widstrand. 1957
         Two editions, because of incompleteness, were withdrawn from sale and destroyed.

0819      **Lolita**. Translated by Nils Holmberg. Stockholm. Bonniers. 1960, 1965

0820      Switzerland: see France. *0802*

0821      Turkey: **Lolita**. Translated by Leylâ Niven. Istanbul. Aydin Yayinevi. 1959

Reprinted: Istanbul. Karaca Yayinevi. 1962
Unauthorized editions, both by the same translator; the second has an unsigned Foreword with the copyright authorization given as "Copyright Ajansma aittir," address: Cagaloglu-Istanbul.

0822      **Lolita**. Translated by Gönül Suveren. Istanbul. Altin Kitaplar Yayineri. 1964

0823      United Arab Republic: (Five unauthorized Arabic editions: one by translators-publishers Jado & Markam Jabri (Éditions Unies), another by distributor-publisher Zouheir Baalbaki (Bureau Commercial d'Impression).)
See also Arabic translation in Israel, *0807*, and in The Lebanon. *0812*

0824      Uruguay: **Lolita**. Montevideo. Diana. 1959
An unauthorized translation.

0825      Yugoslavia: **Lolita**. Translated by Zlatko Crnković. Rijeka. Otokar Kersovani. 1968
In Serbo-Croatian.

0826      **Lolita**. Translated by Janko Moder. Maribor. Založba Obzorja. 1971
In Slovenian.

0827    **SPRING IN FIALTA and Other Stories (VESNA V FIALTE i Drugie Rasskazy)**. New York. The Chekhov Publishing House (Izdatel'stvo imeni Chekhova). 1956. 313pp. Short story collection
Two stories from this collection (*Spring in Fialta* and *Cloud, Castle, Lake*) had previously appeared in the collection **Nine Stories.** *0783*

| | | |
|---|---|---|
| *0828* | *Spring in Fialta (Vesna v Fialta)* | *0979* |
| *0829* | *The Circle (Krug)* | *0962* |
| *0830* | *The Leonardo (Korolyok)* | *0959* |
| *0831* | *Torpid Smoke (Tyazholyj dym)* | *0974* |
| *0832* | *In Memory of L. I. Shigaev (Pamyati L. I. Shigaeva)* | *0969* |
| *0833* | *Visit to a Museum (Poseshchenie muzeya)* | *1002* |
| *0834* | *Recruitment (Nabor)* | *0977* |
| *0835* | *Lik* | *0997* |
| *0836* | *The Annihilation of Tyrants (Istreblenie tiranov)* | *0995* |
| *0837* | *Vasilij Shishkov* | *1007* |
| *0838* | *The Admiralty Needle (Admiraltejskaya igla)* | *0957* |
| *0839* | *Cloud, Castle, Lake (Oblako, ozero, bashnya)* | *0987* |

*0840*    *Lips to Lips (Usta k ustam)*
This story appeared here for the first time. It was
written in December 1931.

| | | |
|---|---|---|
| *0841* | *Ultima Thule* | *0768* |

0842      Germany: **Frühling in Fialta.** Translated by Wassili Berger, Dieter E. Zimmer, Renate Gerhardt, and Rene Drommert. Reinbek. Rowohlt. 1966

> Although the title of the German edition corresponds to the original, they are different collections, the German containing stories taken from **Spring in Fialta** *0827*, **The Eye** *0743*, and **Nabokov's Dozen** *0858*. With a change of title and further changes of contents (listed separately under first appearances) this collection appeared as Gesammelte Erzählungen (1969), with a Foreword and bibliographical notes by Dieter E. Zimmer.

0843      The Netherlands: **Lente in Fialta.** Translated by M. Coutinho. Amsterdam. De Bezige Bij. 1966

> This collection consists of stories taken from **Spring in Fialta** *0827*, and **Nabokov's Dozen.** *0858*.

0844    **PNIN.** Garden City, New York. Doubleday. 1957. 191pp.; and London. Heinemann. 1957. Novel

> Serialized in *The New Yorker*.
> See also Nabokov's Congeries. *1242*

> Reprinted: New York. Avon. 1959, 1969

> Reprinted: Harmondsworth. Penguin. 1960, 1971

> Excerpt (Chapter 3) in Modern Short Stories—The Uses of the Imagination edited by Arthur Mizener. New York. Norton. 1962

> Reprinted: New York. Atheneum. 1964

> Excerpt in Counterparts edited by Gibbon and Gibbons. Sydney. McGraw-Hill Australia. 1969

> Excerpt (Chapter 5) included in Fiction and Analysis edited by Robert Canzoneri and Page Stegner. Glenview, Illinois. Scott, Foresman and Company. 1970

0845      Chile: **Pnin.** Santiago. Editorial del Nuovo Extremo. 1959

0846 Denmark: **Pnin**. Translated by Jørgen Andersen and Vibeke Willumsen. Copenhagen. Gyldendals. 1964
  There was an earlier edition which was destroyed; this is the second edition.

0847 Finland: **Pnin**. Translated by Vappu Roos. Helsinki. Tammi. 1959

0848 France: **Pnin**. Translated by Michel Chrestien. Paris. Gallimard. 1962

  Excerpt translated by Michel Chrestien in Arts. No. 879. Paris. August 1962; and the entire text in La Revue de Paris. Paris. October–December 1962

0849 Germany: **Pnin**. Translated by Curt Meyer-Clason. Reinbek. Rowohlt. 1960, 1965, 1967, 1969

0850 Italy: **Pnin**. Translated by Letizia Ciotti Miller. Milan. Garzanti. 1959

0851 **Pnin**. Translated by Bruno Oddera. Milan. Mondadori. 1967

0852 Japan: **Pnin**. Translated by Kichinosuke Ohasi in Shosetsu-Shincho. Tokyo. April 1971

0853 The Netherlands: **Pnin**. Translated by A. E. Bayer. Amsterdam. Hollandia. 1958

0854 **Pnin**. Translated by Else Hoog. Amsterdam. Uitgeverej De Arbeiderspers. 1968, 1969

0855 Spain: **Pnin**. Translated by Maria Espineira de Monge. Barcelona. Pomaire. 196?

0856            **Pnin.** Translated by Ramon Folch I Camarasa. Barcelona. Edicions 62 S. A. 1968
In Catalan.

0857            Sweden: **Pnin.** Translated by Nils Kjellstrom. Stockholm. Wahlstrom & Widstrand. 1958
Removed from sale and destroyed because of incompleteness.

0858   **NABOKOV'S DOZEN.** New York. Doubleday. 1958. 214pp.; and London. Heinemann. 1959 Short story collection
All but four of these thirteen stories (*First Love, Signs and Symbols, Scenes from the Life of a Double Monster,* and *Lance*) appeared in **Nine Stories.** *0783*

Reprinted: New York. Popular Library. 1958, 1959
This edition was titled **Spring in Fialta.**

Reprinted: Harmondsworth. Penguin Books. 1960, 1971

Reprinted: Freeport, N.Y. Books for the Library Press. 1969

| | | |
|---|---|---|
| 0859 | *Spring in Fialta*<br>Translation of *Vesna v Fialte.* | *0979* |
| 0860 | *A Forgotten Poet* | *1027* |
| 0861 | *First Love* | *1044* |
| 0862 | *Signs and Symbols* | *1039* |
| 0863 | *The Assistant Producer* | *1017* |
| 0864 | *The Aurelian*<br>Translation of *Pil'gram.* *0936* | *0937* |

0865 *Cloud, Castle, Lake*       *0987*
    Translation of *Oblako, ozero, bashnya.* *0839*

0866 *Conversation Piece, 1945*     *1035*
    Entitled *Double Talk* in **Nine Stories.** *0783*

0867 *'That in Aleppo Once. . .'*      *1022*

0868 *Time and Ebb*        *1031*

0869 *Scenes from the Life of a Double Monster* *1052*

0870 *Mademoiselle O*       *1008*

0871 *Lance*          *1049*

0872 Finland: **Nabokovin tusina.** Translated by Eila Pennanen and Juhani Jaskari. Jyväskylä. K. J. Gummerus. 1961

0873 **PALE FIRE.** New York. G. P. Putnam's Sons. 1962; and London. Weidenfeld & Nicolson. 1962. Novel. 315pp.

   Excerpt entitled "The Late Mr. Shade" in Harper's Magazine. New York. May 1962

   Reprinted: New York. Lancer. 1963

   Reprinted: London. Transworld Corgi. 1964–1965, 1966

   Reprinted: New York. Lancer. 1966

   Reprinted: New York. Berkeley Medallion. 1968

   Reprinted: New York. Fawcett Crest. 1970

0874 France: **Feu Pâle.** Translated by Raymond Girard and Edgar Coindreau. Paris. Gallimard. 1965

Excerpt in L'Arc. Aix-en-Provence. February 1964

0875      Germany: **Fahles Feuer.** Translated by Uwe Friesel. Reinbek. Rowohlt. 1968
> Published together with a paperback companion volume "Marginalien" containing the novel's poem in German and English, critical material by A. Field and U. Friesel, and some press quotations.

0876      Italy: **Fuoco Pallido.** Translated by Bruno Oddera. Milan. Mondadori. 1965

0877      Sweden: Excerpt entitled "Pale Fire" ("Blex eld"). Translated by Filippa Rolf. In BLM. February 1966
> "Canto One" of **Pale Fire,** with English text and translator's notes. (It should be noted that there was a certain degree of controversy in the Swedish press over alleged emendations in the text of this translation.)

0878      **NABOKOV'S QUARTET.** New York. Phaedra. 1966; and London. Weidenfeld & Nicolson. 1967. A short story collection

Reprinted: New York. Pyramid. 1968

Reprinted: London. Panther. 1969

| 0879 | *Visit to a Museum* | *1002* |
| 0880 | *Lik* | *0997* |
| 0881 | *An Affair of Honor* | *0933* |
| 0882 | *The Vane Sisters* | *1056* |

0883      Japan: **Shijūso-Me.** Translated by Toyoki Ogasawara. Tokyo. Hakusuisha. 1967
        Published together with **The Eye** through arrangements with Orion Press.

0884    NABOKOV'S CONGERIES and THE PORTABLE NABOKOV
For prose reprinted in these volumes see *1242*.

0885    **ADA OR ARDOR: A FAMILY CHRONICLE.** New York and Toronto. McGraw-Hill. 1969; and London. Weidenfeld & Nicolson. 1969. 589pp.

       Excerpts (Chapters 5–19, Part I) in Playboy. Chicago. 1969
This excerpt deleted two original passages.

       Reprinted: London. Penguin, 1970, 1971

       Reprinted: Fawcett Crest. New York. 1970

0886      Denmark: **Ada, eller Ardor.** Translated by Karen Mathiasen. Copenhagen. Gyldendal. 1971

0887      Finland: **Ada.** Translated by Juhani Jaskari. Jyväskylä. K. J. Gummerus. 1971

0888      Italy: **Ada o dell'Ardore.** Translated by Bruno Oddera. Milan. Mondadori. 1969, 1970

0889      Mexico: **Ada.** Translated by A. Menini Pages. Mexico City. Editorial Grijalbo. 1970

0890      The Netherlands: **Ada; of, Adoratie, een familie kroniek.** Translated by J. F. Kliphuis. Amsterdam. H. Meulenhoff-Baarn. 1970

0891    **A RUSSIAN BEAUTY—NABOKOV'S SECOND DOZEN.** New York. McGraw-Hill. 1973

A collection of Nabokov's Russian stories (1927–1940) translated into English by Dmitri Nabokov and Vladimir Nabokov except for the title story, translated by Simon Karlinsky and Vladimir Nabokov. With the author's forewords. *An Affair of Honor* and *The Visit to the Museum* appeared previously in **Nabokov's Quartet.** See *0878*

| | | |
|---|---|---|
| 0892 | *A Russian Beauty* | *0965* |
| 0893 | *The Leonardo* | *0959* |
| 0894 | *Torpid Smoke* | *0974* |
| 0895 | *Breaking the News* | *0967* |
| 0896 | *Lips to Lips* | *0840* |
| 0897 | *The Visit to the Museum* | *1002* |
| 0898 | *An Affair of Honor* | *0944* |
| 0899 | *Terra Incognita* | *0945* |
| 0900 | *A Dashing Fellow* | *0972* |
| 0901 | *Ultima Thule* | *0768* |
| 0902 | *Solus Rex* | *0768* |

0903   *The Potato Elf*
   A new translation entirely different from the one which appeared in Esquire in 1939. See *0911*.

*0904*    *The Circle*                                    *0962*

*0905*    **TRANSPARENT THINGS.** 1972

# Short Stories:
# Separate Appearances
# and Translations

0906 *Wingstroke* (*Udar kryla*) in Russian Echo (Russkoe Èkho). No. 1. Berlin. January 1924

0907 *Vengeance* (*Mest'*) in Russian Echo (Russkoe Èkho). Berlin. April 20, 1924. pp. 6–8

0908 *Well-Being* (*Blagost'*) in The Rudder (Rul'). Berlin. April 27, 1924. pp. 6–7

0909 *The Port* (*Port*) in The Rudder (Rul'). Berlin. May 24, 1924. pp. 2–3

0910 *The Potato Elf* (*Kartofel'nyj èlf*) in Russian Echo (Russkoe Èkho). Berlin. June 8, 1924. pp. 6–7; June 15, 1924. pp. 5–7; June 22, 1924. pg. 8; June 29, 1924. pp. 6–7

  Reprinted in The Rudder (Rul'). Berlin. December 15, 17–19, 1929. pp. 2–3, 2–3, 2–3, 2

0911 English: *The Potato Elf*. Translated by S. Bertensson and I. Kosinska in Esquire. New York. December 1939. pp. 70–71, 228, 230–236

  Included in The Single Voice edited by Jerome Charyn. New York. Macmillan. 1969

  Excerpt in Composition-Rhetoric edited by Corbet and Burke. New York. Appleton-Century-Crofts. 1971

0912 *Chance Occurrence* (*Sluchajnost'*) in Today (Segodnya). Riga. June 22, 1924. pp. 7–8

0913 *A Catastrophe* (*Katastrofa*) in Today (Segodnya). Riga. July 13, 1924. pp. 5–6

0914 *Bakhman* in The Rudder (Rul'). Berlin. November 2 and 4, 1924. pp. 2–3 and 2–3

*0915*   *The Storm* (*Groza*) in The Rudder (Rul'). Berlin. August 1924?

*0916*       Italy: *Il Temporale* in Narratori Russi Moderni edited by Pietro Zveteremich. Milan. Bompiani. 1963

*0917*   *The Gods* (*Bogi*) in Today (Segodnya). Riga. 1924?

*0918*   *Christmas* (*Rozhdestvo*) in The Rudder (Rul'). Berlin. January 6 and 8, 1925. pp. 2–3 and pg. 2

*0919*   *Letter to Russia* (*Pis'mo v Rossiyu*) in The Rudder (Rul'). Berlin. January 29, 1925. pp. 2–3
         With the notation "from the second chapter of the novel *Happiness* (*Schast'e*)".

*0920*   *The Fight* (*Draka*) in The Rudder (Rul'). Berlin. September 26, 1925. pp. 2–3

*0921*   *The Return of Chorb* (*Vozvrashchenie Chorba*) in The Rudder (Rul'). Berlin. November 12–13, 1925. pp. 2–3 and 2–3

*0922*       English: *The Return of Tchorb*. Translated by Gleb Struve in This Quarter. Vol. 4. No. 4. Paris. June 1932. pp. 592–602

*0923*   *Guidebook to Berlin* (*Putevoditel' po Berlinu*) in The Rudder (Rul'). Berlin. December 24, 1925. pp. 2–3

*0924*       Germany: *Stadtführer durch Berlin*. Translated by Wassili Berger in Neue Deutsche Hefte. Berlin. February 1966

         Reprinted: **Frühling in Fialta.** *0842*

0925    *The Razor* (*Britva*) in The Rudder (Rul'). Berlin. February 19, 1926. pp. 2–3

0926    *A Fable* (*Skazka*) in the Rudder (Rul'). Berlin. June 27 and 29, 1926. pp. 2–3 and 2–3

0927    *The Passenger* (*Passazhir*) in The Rudder (Rul'). Berlin. March 6, 1927. pp. 2–3

0928    English: *The Passenger*. Translated by Gleb Struve in Lovat Dickson's Magazine. Vol. 2. No. 6. London. June 1934. pp. 719–725

        Included, with facing Russian text, in A Century of Russian Prose and Verse from Pushkin to Nabokov edited by O. R. and R. P. Hughes and G. Struve. New York. Harcourt, Brace. 1967

0929    *Terror* (*Uzhas*) in Contemporary Annals (Sovremennye Zapiski). No. 30. Paris. 1927. pp. 214–220

0930    Germany: *Das Grauen* in Das Berliner Tageblatt. Berlin. July 27, 1928
        The translator is unknown.

0931    *The Doorbell* (*Zvonok*) in The Rudder (Rul'). Berlin. 1927?

0932    *A Christmas Story* (*Rozhdestvenskij rasskaz*) in The Rudder (Rul'). Berlin. December 25, 1928. pp. 2–3

0933    *The Scoundrel* [*An Affair of Honour*] (*Podlets*) in The Rudder (Rul'). Berlin. 1928?

0934        English: *An Affair of Honor*. Translated by Dmitri
            Nabokov in The New Yorker. New York. September 3,
            1966

            Reprinted in **Nabokov's Quartet.** *0878*


0935        Germany: *Der Schuft*. Translated by Wassili Berger in
            **Frühling in Fialta.** *0842*


0936    *Pilgram (Pil'gram)* in Contemporary Annals (Sovremennye
        Zapiski). No. 43. Paris. 1930. pp. 191–207


0937        English: *The Aurelian*. Translated by Vladimir Nabokov
            and Peter Pertzov in The Atlantic Monthly. Boston.
            November 1941


0938        Austria: see Germany. *0941*


0939        Finland: *Pilgram*. Translated by Eila Pennanen and
            Juhani Jaskari in **Nabokovin Tusina.** *0872*


0940        France: *Pilgram*. Translated by M. Slonim and S.
            Campaux in Revue de Paris. Paris. July 1959


0941        Germany: *Pilgram*. Translated by Dieter E. Zimmer in
            Frankfurter Allgemeine Zeitung. Frankfurt. October
            2–3, 1965

            Included in **Frühling in Fialta.** *0842*

            Included in Zuhause. No. 8. Hamburg. August 1967

            Reprinted in Die Presse. Vienna. September 13, 1969


0942        The Netherlands: *Prikkebeen*. Translated by M. Coutinho
            in **Lente in Fialta.** *0843*

0943    *The Offense* (*Obida*) in The Latest News (Poslednie Novosti).
Paris. July 12, 1931. pp. 2–3

0944    *The Busy Man* (*Zanyatoj chelovek*) in The Latest News
(Poslednie Novosti). Paris. October 20, 1931. pp. 2–3
Written between September 17 and 26, 1931

0945    *Terra incognita* in The Latest News (Poslednie Novosti). Paris.
November 22, 1931. pp. 2–3

0946    English: *Terra incognita*. Translated by Dmitri Nabokov
in The New Yorker. New York. May 18, 1963

0947    Bolivia: *Terra incognita* in Arco. La Paz. 1963–65(?)
The publication data obtained for this translation
proved inaccurate, and the correct date of publication has not yet been determined.

0948    Germany: *Terra incognita*. Translated by Dieter E.
Zimmer in **Frühling in Fialta**. *0842*

0949    *The Meeting* (*Vstrecha*) in The Latest News (Poslednie
Novosti). Paris. January 1, 1932. pp. 2–3
The issue number for this appearance, of which there
is some doubt as to the exact date, is No. 3936.

0950    *Goosefoot* (*Lebeda*) in The Latest News (Poslednie Novosti).
Paris. January 31, 1932. pp. 2–3
Written between September 1931 and January 14, 1932.

Reprinted in The Day of the Russian Child (Den' russkogo
rebyonka). New York. April 1942.

0951    *Music* (*Muzyka*) in The Latest News (Poslednie Novosti).
Paris. March 27, 1932. pg. 2

0952   Austria: see Germany. *0955*

0953   France: *Musique*. Translated by Vladimir Nabokov in Les Nouvelles littéraires. Paris. May 14, 1959

0954   Germany: *Musik*. Translated by I. Amdurski-Schubert in Kölnische Zeitung. Cologne. January 7, 1933

     *Musik*. Translated by Dieter E. Zimmer in **Frühling in Fialta.** *0842*

     Reprinted in Arbeiter-Zeitung. Vienna. September 11, 1966

     Reprinted in Westdeutsche Allgemeine Zeitung. Essen. April 19, 1969

     Reprinted in Mannheimer Morgen. Mannheim. April 26, 1969

0956  *Perfection* (*Sovershenstvo*) in The Latest News (Poslednie Novosti). Paris. July 3, 1932. pp. 2–3
    Written June 1932

0957  *The Admiralty Needle* (*Admiraltejskaya igla*) in The Latest News (Poslednie Novosti). Paris. June 4–5, 1933. pg. 3 and pg. 2

0958   Germany: *Die Nadel der Admiralität*. Translated by Wassili Berger in **Frühling in Fialta.** *0842*

     Reprinted in Merkur. Munich. February 1966

0959  *The Leonardo* (*Korolyok*) in The Latest News (Poslednie Novosti). Paris. July 23–24, 1933. pg. 6 and pg. 2

0960   English: Translated for the first time in the collection **A Russian Beauty.** *0894*

0961        Germany: *Der neue Nachbar*. Translated by Wassili Berger in **Frühling in Fialta.** *0842*

0962        *The Circle (Krug)* in The Latest News (Poslednie Novosti). Paris. March 11–12, 1934. pg. 3 and pg. 3

0963        English: *The Circle*. Translated by Dmitri and Vladimir Nabokov in The New Yorker. November, 1971

0964        Sweden: *Cirkeln*. Translated by Staffan Dahl in Modern Rysk Berattarkonst. Stockholm. Aldus Bonniers. 1965

0965    *The Beauty [A Russian Beauty] (Krasavitsa)* in The Latest News (Poslednie Novosti). Paris. August 18, 1934. pg. 2

0966        English: Translated for the first time as the title story of the collection **A Russian Beauty.** *0891*

0967    *Breaking the News (Opoveshchenie)*

0968        English: *Breaking the News*. Translated by Dmitri Nabokov and Vladimir Nabokov in Audience. New York. March, 1972
           This story has been referred to in print as *Notification*.

0969    *In Memory of L. I. Shigaev (Pamyati L. I. Shigaeva)* in either The Rudder (Rul'). Berlin. 1931 or The Latest News (Poslednie Novosti). Paris. 1934
           The date for this story has not been ascertained, and both possible places of publication represent speculation based on vague memory.

0970        Austria: see Germany. *0971*

0971       Germany: *Dem Andenken L. I. Schigajews.* Translated by Rene Drommert in **Frühling in Fialta,** *0842*

Reprinted in Die Presse. Vienna. October 3, 1970


0972   *A Dashing Fellow (Khvat)* in The Latest News (Poslednie Novosti). Paris. 1932?, 1934?
The date of the first appearance of *A Dashing Fellow* is merely speculation.


0973       English: *A Dashing Fellow.* Translated by Dmitri Nabokov and Vladimir Nabokov in Playboy. Chicago. December 1971


0974   *Torpid Smoke (Tyazhyolyj dym)* in The Latest News (Poslednie Novosti). Paris. March 3, 1935. pg. 3


0975       English: *Torpid Smoke.* Translated by Dmitri Nabokov and Vladimir Nabokov in Tri-Quarterly. Evanston, Illinois. 1972


0976       Germany: *Der schwere Rauch.* Translated by Wassili Berger in **Frühling in Fialta.** *0842*

Reprinted in Mannheimer Morgen. Mannheim. September 26, 1970


0977   *Recruitment (Nabor)* in The Latest News (Poslednie Novosti). Paris. August 18, 1935


0978   *An Event from Life (Sluchaj iz zhizni)* in The Latest News (Poslednie Novosti). Paris. September 22, 1935. pg. 3


0979   *Spring in Fialta (Vesna v Fialte)* in Contemporary Annals (Sovremennye Zapiski). No. 61. Paris. 1936. pp. 91–113

0980      English: *Spring in Fialta*. Translated by Vladimir Nabokov and Peter Pertzov in Harper's Bazaar. New York. May 1947

                Included in More Stories Strange and Sinister edited by Laurette Pizer. London. Panther. 1967

0981      Czechoslovakia: *Jaro v Fialtě*. Translated by L. Dušková in Světová Literatura. No. 4. Prague. 1969

0982      Finland: *Fialtan Kevät*. Translated by Eila Pennanen and Juhani Jaskari in **Nabokovin Tusina.** *0872*

0983      France: *Le printemps à Fialta*. Translated by Yves Berger in Les Vingt Meilleures Nouvelles Russes edited by Alain Bosquet. Paris. Seghers. 1960, 1964

0984      Germany: *Frühling in Fialta*. Translated by Dieter E. Zimmer in **Frühling in Fialta.** *0842*

0985      The Netherlands: *Lente in Fialta*. Translated by M. Coutinho in **Lente in Fialta.** *0843*

0986      Spain: *Primavera en Fialta*. Translated by Irene Peypoch in Las Majores Historias Siniestras, $4^e$ Antologia edited by Laurette Pizer. Barcelona. Bruguera. 1967

0987      *Cloud, Castle, Lake (Oblako, ozero, bashnya)* in Russian Annals (Russkie Zapiski). No. 2. Paris. 1937 pp. 33–42

0988      English: *Cloud, Castle, Lake*. Translated by Vladimir Nabokov and Peter Pertzov in The Atlantic Monthly. Boston. June 1941

Included in Modern Tradition: An Anthology of Short Stories edited by D. F. Howard. Boston. Little, Brown. 1968

0989    Denmark: *Selskabsrejsen.* Translated by Elisabeth Rasmussen in Magasinet. Copenhagen. July 18, 1959

0990    Finland: *Pilvi, Linna, Järvi.* Translated by Eila Pennanen and Juhani Jaskari in **Nabokovin Tusina.** *0872*

0991    France: *Le nuage, le lac, le château.* Translated by Vladimir Sikorskij in L'Arc. Aix-en-Provence. February 1964

0992    Germany: *Wolke, Burg, See.* Translated by Renate Gerhardt in Die Zeit. No. 21. Hamburg. 1961

Reprinted: Volksrecht. Zurich. December 11, 1965

0993    The Netherlands: *Wolk, burcht, meer.* Translated by M. Coutinho in **Lente in Fialta.** *0843*

0994    Switzerland: see Germany. *0992*

0995    *The Annihilation of Tyrants* (*Iztreblenie tiranov*) in Russian Annals (Russkie Zapiski). Paris. August–September 1938. pp. 3–29

0996    France: *L'extermination des tyrans.* Translated by Vladimir Sikorskij in Mercure de France. Paris. March 1964

0997    *Lik* in Russian Annals (Russkie Zapiski). Paris. February 1939. pp. 3–27

0998      English: *Lik*. Translated by Dmitri Nabokov in The New Yorker. New York. October 10, 1964

         Included in **Nabokov's Dozen.** *0858*

0999      Colombia: *Lik*. In Eco. Volume 10, No. 60. Bogotá. April 1965
         The translator is not given.

1000      Czechoslovakia: *Sličný*. Translated by L. Dušková in Světová Literaturá. No. 4. Prague. 1969

1001      Germany: *Lik*. Translated by Dieter E. Zimmer in **Frühling in Fialta.** *0842*

1002      *Visit to a Museum (Poseshchenie muzeya)* in Contemporary Annals (Sovremennye Zapiski). No. 68. Paris. 1939. pp. 76–86

1003      English: *The Visit to the Museum*. Translated by Dmitri Nabokov in Esquire. New York. March 1963

         Included in The Dream Adventure edited by Roger Caillois. New York. Orion Press. 1963
         This anthology is a translation of the French anthology Puissances du rêve mentioned below.

         Included in **Nabokov's Quartet**—*0878* and **A Russian Beauty**—*0891*

1004      Argentina: *La visite au musée*. Translated by V. Macarow in Les Lettres françaises. No. 13. Buenos Aires. July 1, 1944

1005      France: *La visite au musée*. Translated by M. and Mme. Cannac in Puissances du rêve edited by Roger Callois. Paris. Le Club Français du Livre. 1962
         See also Argentina.

1006    Germany: *Der Museumsbesuch*. Translated by Dieter E. Zimmer in Die Zeit. No. 12. Hamburg. 1964; and in **Frühling in Fialta.** *0842*

1007    *Vasily Shishkov* in The Latest News (Poslednie Novosti). Paris. 1939
        A more precise date of appearance for this short story has not been established.

1008    *Mademoiselle O* in Mesures. Paris. 1939
        The original version, written in French. This is actually a memoir; see **Speak, Memory.** *1096*

1009    English: *Mademoiselle O.* Translated by Vladimir Nabokov and Hilda Ward in The Atlantic Monthly. Boston. January 1943

        Included in Varieties of Prose edited by G. Perkins. Glenview, Illinois. Scott, Foresman. 1966

        Excerpt in Matters of Style by J. Mittchell Morse. New York. Bobbs-Merrill. 1968

1010    Argentina: *Mademoiselle O.* Translated by Edgardo Cozarinsky in Sur. Buenos Aires.
        The publication date originally obtained (1965) proved inaccurate. The proper one has not yet been determined.

1011    Finland: *Mademoiselle O.* Translated by Eila Pennanen in **Nabokovin Tusina.** *0872*

1012    The Netherlands: *Mademoiselle O.* Translated by M. Coutinho in **Lente in Fialta.** *0843*

1013    *Solus Rex*—See *0768*

1014      English: *Solus Rex*. Translated for the first time in **A Russian Beauty.** *0891*

1015    *Ultima Thule*—See *0768*

1016      English: *Ultima Thule*. Translated by Dmitri Nabokov and Vladimir Nabokov in The New Yorker. New York. 1972

1017    *The Assistant Producer* in The Atlantic Monthly. Boston. May 1943. pp. 68–74

        Included in Great Spy Stories from Fiction edited by Allen W. Dulles. New York. Harper & Row. 1969

1018      Finland: *Apulaisohjaaja*. Translated by Eila Pennanen and Juhani Jaskari in **Nabokovin Tusina.** *0872*

1019      Germany: *Der Regieassistent*. Translated by Dieter E. Zimmer in **Frühling in Fialta.** *0842*

1020      Italy: Included in Grandi Storie di Spie. Translated by Antonia Rerrigan. Garzanti. 1971

1021      The Netherlands: *De assistent-regisseur*. Translated by M. Coutinho in **Lente in Fialta.** *0843*

1022    'That in Aleppo Once . . .' in The Atlantic Monthly. Boston. November 1943. pp. 88–92

        Included in The Best American Short Stories, 1944 edited by Martha Foley. Boston. Houghton Mifflin. 1944

        Included in The Great Psychological Stories edited by L. N. Pizer. London. Panther. 1967

Included in Short Stories, Classic, Modern, Contemporary edited by Marcus Klein and Robert Pack. Boston. Little, Brown. 1968

Included in The Shape of Fiction edited by Leo Hamalian and Frederick Karl. New York. McGraw-Hill. 1967

Included in The Modern Tradition: An Anthology of Short Stories edited by D. F. Howard. Boston. Little, Brown. 1968

Included in Reading for Understanding edited by Caroline Shrodes, Justine Van Grundy and Joel Dorius. New York. Macmillan. 1968

Included in American Literature edited by R. Poirier et al. Volume 2. Boston. Little, Brown. 1970

*1023*    Finland: *'Että Kerran Aleppossa.'* Translated by Eila Pennanen and Juhani Jaskari in **Nabokovin Tusina.** *0872*

*1024*    France: in Mercure de France. Paris. Further data on this appearance has not yet been obtained.

*1025*    Germany: *'das in Aleppo einst.'* Translated by Dieter E. Zimmer in Die Zeit. No. 49. Hamburg. 1965

Reprinted in **Frühling in Fialta.** *0842*

*1026*    The Netherlands: *'Eens, in Aleppo.'* Translated by M. Coutinho in **Lente in Fialta.** *0843*

*1027*  *A Forgotten Poet* in The Atlantic Monthly. Boston. October 1944. pp. 60–65

*1028*    Finland: *Unohdettu Runoilija.* Translated by Eila Pennanen and Juhani Jaskari in **Nabokovin Tusina.** *0872*

1029      Germany: *Ein vergessener Dichter*. Translated by Dieter E. Zimmer in **Frühling in Fialta.** *0842*

1030      The Netherlands: *Een vergeten dichter*. Translated by M. Coutinho in **Lente in Fialta.** *0843*

1031      *Time and Ebb* in The Atlantic Monthly. Boston. January 1945. pp. 81–84

         Included in The Best American Short Stories, 1946 edited by Martha Foley. Boston. Houghton Mifflin. 1946

1032      Finland: *Vuodet ja Luode*. Translated by Eila Pennanen and Juhani Jaskari in **Nabokovin Tusina.** *0872*

1033      Germany: *Zeit und Ebbe*. Translated by Dieter E. Zimmer in **Frühling in Fialta.** *0842*

1034      The Netherlands: *Tij en wantij*. Translated by M. Coutinho in **Lente in Fialta.** *0843*

1035      *Double Talk* in The New Yorker. New York. June 23, 1945. pp. 20–25
         Later re-titled *Conversation Piece, 1945*

1036      Finland: *Seurustelukuva*. Translated by Eila Pennanen and Juhani Jaskari in **Nabokovin Tusina.** *0872*

1037      Germany: *Genrebild 1945*. Translated by Dieter E. Zimmer in **Frühling in Fialta.** *0842*

1038      The Netherlands: *Informele portretgroep*. Translated by M. Coutinho in **Lente in Fialta.** *0843*

1039    *Signs and Symbols* in The New Yorker. New York. May 15, 1948. pp. 31–32

Included in Honey and Wax—The Powers and Pleasures of Narrative edited by Richard Stern. Chicago. University of Chicago Press. 1966

Included in Short Stories—Classic, Modern Contemporary edited by Marcus Klein and Robert Pack. Boston. Little, Brown. 1967

Included in Anthology of the Short Story edited by Robert C. Albrecht. Free Press—Macmillan. New York. 1969


1040    Austria: see Germany. *1042*


1041    Finland: *Merkkejä ja Symboleja.* Translated by Eila Pennanen and Juhani Jaskari in **Nabokovin Tusina.** *0872*


1042    Germany: *Zeichen und Symbole.* Translated by Renate Gerhardt in Heute. Vienna. June 11, 1960

Reprinted in Stuttgarter Zeitung. Stuttgart. December 18, 1965

Included in **Frühling in Fialta.** *0842*

Included in Christl von der Post. No. 6. Bonn. June 1970

Included in Bremer Nachrichten. Bremen. October 3, 1970

Included in Die Zeit. No. 16. Hamburg. 1970


1043    The Netherlands: *Signalen en symbolen.* Translated by M. Coutinho in **Lente in Fialta.** *0843*


1044    *Colette* in The New Yorker. New York. July 31, 1948
Later re-titled *First Love* (see **Nabokov's Dozen.** *0858*), this piece is actually a section of Nabokov's memoirs, see **Speak, Memory.** *1096*

1045     *First Love* included in Love Around the World. New York. Berkeley Publishing Corporation. 1959

Included in The Tastes of Love edited by Denys Baker. London. New English Library. 1962

Included in The Modern Tradition edited by D. F. Howard. Boston. Little, Brown. 1968

Included in The Art of a Story, an Introduction edited by Robert Hollander and Sidney E. Lind. New York. American Book Company. 1968

Excerpt in Matters of Style by J. Mittchell Morse. New York. Bobbs-Merrill. 1968


1046     Denmark: *Den første kaerlighed*. Translated by Elisabeth Rasmussen in Magasinet. Copenhagen. August 29, 1959


1047     Finland: *Ensirakkaus*. Translated by Eila Pennanen and Juhani Jaskari in **Nabokovin Tusina.** *0872*


1048     The Netherlands: *Eerste liefde*. Translated by M. Coutinho in **Lente in Fialta.** *0843*


1049  *Lance* in The New Yorker. New York. February 2, 1952. pp. 21–55

Included in Stories from the New Yorker 1950–1960. New York. Simon & Schuster. 1960; and London. Victor Gollancz. 1961; and London. Penguin. 1963

Included in A College Treasury edited by Paul Jorgenson and Frederick Shroyer. New York. Charles Scribner. n.d.


1050     Finland: *Lancelot*. Translated by Eila Pennanen and Juhani Jaskari in **Nabokovin Tusina.** *0872*


1051     Germany: *Lance*. Translated by Dieter E. Zimmer in Merkur. No. 171. Munich. 1962

Reprinted in **Frühling in Fialta.**  *0842*

1052    *Scenes from the Life of a Double Monster* in The Reporter. New York. March 20, 1958. pp. 34–37

    Included in Black Humor edited by Bruce Jay Friedman. New York. Bantam Books. 1965

1053    Argentina: *Escenas de la vida de un monstruo doble.* Translated by Edgardo Cozarinsky in Sur. No. 271. Buenos Aires. July–August 1961

1054    Germany: *Szenen aus dem Leben eines Doppelungeheuers.* Translated by Dieter E. Zimmer in **Frühling in Fialta.**  *0842*

1055    The Netherlands: *Taferelen uit het leven van een tweevondig monster.* Translated by M. Coutinho in **Lente in Fialta.**  *0843*

1056    *The Vane Sisters* in Hudson Review. New York. Vol. 11. No. 4. Winter 1959

    Also in Encounter. London. March 1959. pp. 3–10

    Included in The Modern Image—Outstanding Stories from the Hudson Review edited by Frederick Morgan. Boston. Little, Brown. 1965

    Included in The Short Story: An Introductory Anthology edited by Robert Rees and Barry Menikoff. Boston. Little, Brown. 1969

    Included in Great Short Stories from the World's Literature edited by Charles Neider. New York. Holt, Reinhart & Winston. 1970

    Included in Studies in Short Fiction edited by D. Hughes. New York. Holt, Reinhart & Winston. 1970

1057    Czechoslovakia: (Translated title and translator un-
        known) in Revue Svetovej Literatury. Bratislava. 1968

1058    France: *Les Soeurs Vane*. Translated by Roger Giroux
        in Les Lettres nouvelles. Paris. May 13, 1959

1059    Germany: *Die Schwestern Vane*. Translated by Dieter E.
        Zimmer in Süddeutsche Zeitung. Munich. January 15,
        1966

1060    Sweden: *Systarna Vane*. Translated by Sonja Bergvall
        in BLM med AVB. Stockholm. April 1959

1061    *The Magician*. Excerpts translated by A. Field in Nabokov—
        His Life in Art. Boston. Little, Brown. 1967. pp. 328–329
        Two excerpts from the unpublished Russian short story
        *Volshebnik* (1939) which was the precursor to **Lolita.**

1062    *Lips to Lips*. Translated by Dmitri Nabokov in Esquire. New      *0840*
        York. November 1971

# Plays and Scenarios

1063    **Death (Smert')** in The Rudder (Rul'). Berlin. May 20 and 24, 1923. pg. 13; 5–6

        A verse drama in two acts.


1064    **Grand-dad (Dedushka)** in The Rudder (Rul'). Berlin. October 14, 1923

        A one-act play. Written June 30, 1923. pp. 5–6


1065    **Agaspher (Agasfer)** in The Rudder (Rul'). Berlin. December 2, 1923. pg. 6

        A dramatic monologue written as a prologue to a staged symphony.


1066    **The Wanderers (Skital'tsy)** in Facets II (Grani II). Berlin. 1923

        A supposed translation of the first act of a play by the non-existant English author "Vivian Calmbrood."


1067    **The Tragedy of Mister Morn (Tragediya Gospodina Morna)** in The Rudder (Rul'). Berlin. April 6, 1924

        A plot précis given on the basis of a reading and short excerpts from this otherwise unpublished five-act play are incorporated in an article in The Rudder. See *1399*


1068    **The South Pole (Polyus)** in the Rudder (Rul'). Berlin. August 14 and 16, 1924. pp. 2–3; 2–3

        A verse drama in one act.


1069    **The Man From The USSR (Chelovek Iz SSSR)** in the Rudder (Rul'). Berlin. January 1, 1927

        Only the first act of this five-act play appeared in print; it was staged in Berlin in 1926.


1070    **The Event (Sobytie)** in Russian Annals (Russkie Zapiski). No. 4. Paris. April 1938. pp. 43–104

        A dramatic comedy in three acts. Staged in Paris and Prague, May 1938: in Warsaw, Belgrade and New York, 1941

**1071**   **The Waltz Invention (Izobretenie val'sa)** in Russian Annals
(Russkie Zapiski). Paris. November 1938. pp. 3–62
A drama in three acts. Staged, in Russian, at Oxford
University in Spring, 1968.

**1072**   English: **The Waltz Invention.** Translated by Dmitri
Nabokov. New York. Phaedra. 1966

Reprinted: New York. Pocket Books. 1967

Staged in Connecticut. 1969

**1073**   The Netherlands: **De Uitvinding Van Wals.** Translated by
Cees Nooteboom. Amsterdam. De Bezige Bij. 1971

**1074**   Spain: **Vals y su Invencion.**
Further information is lacking.

**1075**   **Rusalka.** New York. 1942
A dramatic poem. See *0600*

**1076**   **Lolita.** New York. McGraw-Hill. 1974
Screenplay for the 1962 MGM film of the novel, differing
in many respects from the scenario that was used.

1077    *Mademoiselle O* in The Atlantic Monthly. Boston. January 1943
         Chapter 5 of **Speak, Memory.** *1096.* This piece was origi-
         nally published as a short story.


1078    *Portrait of My Uncle* in The New Yorker. New York. January
        3, 1948
         Chapter 3 of **Speak, Memory.** *1096*


1079    *My English Education* in The New Yorker. New York. March
        27, 1948
         Chapter 4 of **Speak, Memory.** *1096*


1080    *Butterflies* in The New Yorker. New York. July 31, 1948
         Chapter 6 of **Speak, Memory.** *1096*

         Included in Intention and Choice edited by Gregory T.
         Polletta. New York. Random House. 1967

         Included in Structure in Composition edited by Eileen Rall
         and Karl Snyder. Scott, Foresman and Company. 1970


1081    *Colette* in The New Yorker. New York. July 31, 1948
         Chapter 7 of **Speak, Memory.** *1096.* This piece was origi-
         nally published as a short story. *1044.*


1082    *My Russian Education* in The New Yorker. New York. Sep-
        tember 18, 1948
         Chapter 9 of **Speak, Memory.** *1096.* (An addition to this
         chapter appeared in The New Leader. New York. May 9,
         1966; it was incorporated in **Speak, Memory—An Auto-
         biography Revisited** [*1104*] and was subsequently re-
         printed as an Afterword to The Provisional Government
         by V. D. Nabokov. Brisbane. University of Queensland
         Press. 1970. pp. 123–127)


1083    *Curtain Raiser* in The New Yorker. New York. January 1,
        1949
         Chapter 10 of **Speak, Memory.** *1096*

1084  *Portrait of My Mother* in The New Yorker. New York. April
      9, 1949
          Chapter 2 of **Speak, Memory.**  *1096*


1085  *First Poem* in Partisan Review. New York. September 1949
          Chapter 11 of **Speak, Memory.**  *1096*


1086  Bolivia: *Mi primer poema* in Arco. La Paz. (?).
          The particulars of this listing have proved in error.


1087  Germany: *Mein erstes Gedicht.* Translated by Dieter E.
          Zimmer in Merkur. Munich. June 1963


1088  *Tamara* in The New Yorker. New York. December 10, 1949
          Chapter 12 of **Speak, Memory.**  *1096*


1089  *Lantern Slides* in The New Yorker. New York. February 11,
      1950
          Chapter 8 of **Speak, Memory.**  *1096*


1090  *Perfect Past* in The New Yorker. New York. April 15, 1950
          Chapter 1 of **Speak, Memory.**  *1096*


1091  *Gardens and Parks* in The New Yorker. New York. June 17,
      1950
          Chapter 15 of **Speak, Memory.**  *1096*

      Included in American Literature edited by Richard Poirier.
      Boston. Little, Brown. 1970.


1092  *Lodgings in Trinity Lane* in Harper's Magazine. New York.
      January 1951
          Chapter 13 of **Speak, Memory.**  *1096*


1093  *Exile* in Partisan Review. New York. January–February 1951

*1094*   Italy: *Esilio.* Translated by Luigi Berti in Inventario. Vol. 4. No. 1. Milan. January–February 1952

*1095*   **CONCLUSIVE EVIDENCE—A MEMOIR.** New York. Harper & Brothers. 1951. 240pp.
This book was later re-titled **Speak, Memory.** *1096*

*1096*   **SPEAK, MEMORY.** London. Victor Gollancz. 1951
This is **Conclusive Evidence** re-titled but unchanged. *1095.*

Reprinted: New York. Grosset & Dunlop. 1960

Excerpt in The Open Forum—Essays for Our Time edited by Alfred Kazin. New York. Harcourt, Brace. 1961

Excerpt in Using Prose edited by W. Moynihan and D. W. Lee. New York. Dodd-Mead. 1966

Excerpt in The Relevance of Rhetoric edited by E. V. Stackpoole and W. R. Winterowd. Boston. Allyn & Bacon. 1966

Reprinted: See *1104*

Excerpt in Autobiography edited by Maurianne Adams. Indianapolis. Bobbs-Merrill. 1967

Excerpt in The Magic of Walking edited by A. Sussman and R. Goode. New York. Simon & Schuster. 1967

Excerpt in Varieties of Prose edited by G. Polletta. New York. Random House. 1967

Excerpt in Narrative Argument edited by D. Knapp. New York. McGraw-Hill. 1967

Excerpt in Matters of Style edited by J. Mittchell Morse. Indianapolis. Bobbs-Merrill. 1968

Reprinted: New York. Pyramid. 1968, 1970

Reprinted: London. Penguin. 1969

Excerpt in As Up They Grew: Autobiographical Essays edited by Herbert R. Coursen. Glenview, Illinois. Scott, Foresman and Company. 1970

1097  Russian: **Other Shores (Drugie Berega).** Translated and revised by Vladimir Nabokov. New York. Chekhov Publishing House (Izdatel'stvo imeni Chekhova). 1954. 266pp.
This edition contains numerous remarks and more detailed passages for the benefit of the author's Russian-speaking readers.

Serialized in Essays (Opyty). No. 3. New York. 1954. (Chapters 1–3); and New Review (Novyj Zhurnal). No. 37. (Chapters 4–6) and No. 38 (Chapters 7–9). New York. 1954

1098  Denmark: **My European Youth (Min Europaeiske ungdom).** Translated by Peter Nørgaard and Morten Piil. Copenhagen. Gyldendal. 1969

1099  France: **Autres Rivages.** Translated by Yvonne Davet. Paris. Gallimard. 1961

1100  Germany: **Andere Ufer.** Translated by Dieter E. Zimmer. Reinbek. Rowohlt. 1964
The translation was made from the English text but borrowed the Russian title.

Excerpt (Chapters 1, 2, 7 and 13). Translated by Dieter E. Zimmer in Neue Zürcher Zeitung. November 26–December 8, 1963

1101  Italy: **Parla, ricordo.** Translated by Bruno Oddera. Milan. Mondadori. 1962

1102  The Netherlands: **Geheugen, spreek.** Translated by M. and L. Coutinho. Amsterdam. De Bezige Bij-Meulenhoff. 1968

*1103*     Spain: **Habla, memoria!** Translated by Jaime Pineiro Gonzalez. Barcelona. Plaza & Janes. 1963

*1104*   **SPEAK, MEMORY—AN AUTOBIOGRAPHY REVISITED.** New York. G. P. Putnam's Sons. 1967; and London. Weidenfeld & Nicolson. 1967
A new, revised and enlarged edition, illustrated with seventeen family photographs, a plate with butterflies, and endpapers by the author depicting the pre-revolutionary Nabokov properties. This edition should be regarded as an evolved version of **Conclusive Evidence** and **Other Shores.**

*1105*   **SPEAK ON, MEMORY.** 1975?
N. B. Although the continuation of his memoirs has been referred to under the title Speak On, Memory for many years in interviews, Nabokov has in recent times been calling the book Speak, America.

# Essays,
# Book Reviews,
# and Criticism

1106    *Cambridge (Kèmbridzh)* in The Rudder (Rul'). Berlin. October 28, 1921. pg. 2

1107    *Rupert Brooke* in Facets I (Grani I). Berlin. 1922. pp. 213–31

1108    Review of poems by Sergei Krechetov (An Iron Ring [Zheleznyj persten']) in The Rudder (Rul'). Berlin. December 17, 1922. pg. 11

1109    *The Enchanted Nightingale, a tale by Richard Dehmal (Volshebnyj Solovej, skazka Richard Demmelya).* Review of a fable, The Enchanted Nightingale by Richard Dehmal as translated by Sasha Chyorny, in The Rudder (Rul'). Berlin. March 30, 1924. pg. 7

1110    *Aleksandr Saltykov: Odes and Hymns (Aleksandr Saltykov: Ody i Gimny).* Review of Odes and Hymns by Aleksandr Saltykov in The Rudder (Rul'). Berlin. October 1, 1924. pg. 5

1111    Review of poems by A. Bulkin in The Rudder (Rul'). Berlin. August 25, 1926

1112    Review of poems by B. Dukel'sky (Sonnets [Sonety]) in The Rudder (Rul'). Berlin. November 3, 1926

1113    Review of poems by Sergei Rafalovich in The Rudder (Rul'). Berlin. January 19, 1927

1114    Review of poems by D. Kobyakov (Bitter Stuff [Gorech'] and Ceramics [Keramika]) and E. Shakh (The Seed on the Stone [Semya na Kamne]) in The Rudder (Rul'). Berlin. May 11, 1927. pg. 4

1115    Review of a chess book, Capablanca and Alekhin, by A. Znosko-Borovsky in The Rudder (Rul'). Berlin. November 16, 1927

1116    *Jubilee* (*Yubilej*) in The Rudder (Rul'). Berlin. November 18, 1927
    A political article.

1117    English: Excerpts translated by A. Field in Nabokov—His Life in Art. Boston. Little, Brown. 1967

1118    Review of a Belgrade almanac The Architect (Zodchij) in The Rudder (Rul'). Berlin. November 23, 1927
    This article contains reviews of poems by V. S. Grigorovich, E. Kiskevich, I. Kondratovich, E. Tauber, A. Kostyuk, L. Kremelev, L. Mashkovsky, G. Nalench, D. Sidorov, and Yu. Sopotsko.

1119    Review of poems by Andrei Blokh (Poems [Stikhi]) in The Rudder (Rul'). Berlin. November 30, 1927

1120    *New Poets* (*Novye poèty*) in The Rudder (Rul'). Berlin. November 31, 1927. pg. 4
    A review of poems by V. Dixon, D. Gusev, R. Arkadin, L. Shlossberg, Iu. Galich, and G. Pronin.

1121    Review of poems by Vladislav Khodasevich (Collected Poems [Sobranie stikhov]) in The Rudder (Rul'). Berlin. December 14, 1927

1122    Review of poems by Raisa Blokh (My City [Moj Gorod]) and Maryam Stoyam (Ham [Kham]) in The Rudder (Rul'). Berlin. March 7, 1928. pg. 4

1123    *Three Books of Poetry* (*Tri knigi stikhov*) in The Rudder (Rul'). Berlin. May 22, 1928. pg. 4

A review of poems by B. Bozhnev and D. Knut and of the collection The Poem: Poetry and Poetic Criticism (Stikhotvorenie: Poèziya i poeticheskaya kritika).

1124 *Omar-Khayyam in Ivan Tkhorzhevsky's Translation* (*Omar-Khayam v perevodakh Iv. Tkhorzhevskogo*) in The Rudder (Rul'). Berlin. May 29, 1928. pg. 4
A review of I. Tkhorzhevsky's translations of Omar Khayyam.

1125 Review of An Anthology of Lunar Poets (Antologiya Lunnykh Poètov) in The Rudder (Rul'). Berlin. June 6, 1928. pg. 4

1126 Brief corrective note in The Rudder (Rul'). Berlin. June 20, 1928
The note concerns a misprint in a review of Dovid Knut's poetry.

1127 *Two Slavic Poets* (*Dva slavyanskikh poèta*) in The Rudder (Rul'). Berlin. October 10, 1928
A review of poems by N. Beskid and J. Kasprovich.

1128 Review of poems by V. Pozner (Chance Poems [Stikhi na Sluchaj]) and N. Snesareva-Kazakova (Blessed Be Your Name [Da Svyatitsya Imya Tvoyo]) in The Rudder (Rul'). Berlin. October 24, 1928. pg. 4

1129 *An Exhibition of M. Nakhman-Achariya* (*Vystavka M. Nakhman-Achariya*) in The Rudder (Rul'). Berlin. October 31, 1928
A review of an exhibition of paintings.

1130 Review of the collection of fables The Star Above Stars (Zvezda Nadzvezdnaya) by A. Remizov in The Rudder (Rul'). Berlin. November 11, 1928. pg. 4

1131    *In Memory of Yu. Aikhenval'd* (*Pamyati Yu. I. Aikhenval'da*)
        in The Rudder (Rul'). Berlin. December 23, 1928. pg. 5


1132    Review of Contemporary Annals No. 37 (Sovremennye Zapiski
        XXXVII) in The Rudder (Rul'). Berlin. February 2, 1929.
        pg. 2


1133    Review of the Prague journal The Will of Russia (Volya Rossii).
        No. 2 (1929) in The Rudder (Rul'). Berlin. May 8, 1929.
        pg. 4


1134    *A Literary Review* (*Literaturnoe obozrenie*). A review of
        Selected Poems (Izbrannye Stikhi) by Ivan Bunin in The
        Rudder (Rul'). Berlin. May 22, 1929. pp. 2–3


1135    Review of stories by A. Damanskaya (Wives [Zhyony]) in The
        Rudder (Rul'). Berlin. September 25, 1929. pg. 5


1136    Review of a short story collection, Èlan', by A. Kuprin in The
        Rudder (Rul'). Berlin. October 23, 1929. pg. 5


1137    Review of a novel, Iseult (Izolda), by I. Odoevtseva in The
        Rudder (Rul'). Berlin. October 30, 1929. pg. 5


1138    *With Red Feet* (*Na krasnykh lapkakh*) in The Rudder (Rul').
        Berlin. January 29, 1930
            A critique of an article by Aleksei Eisner in The Will of
        Russia attacking Bunin's poetry.


1139    *The Triumph of Virtue* (*Torzhestvo Dobrodeteli*) in The Rud-
        der (Rul'). Berlin. March 5, 1930. pp. 2–3
            A satirical article about Soviet literature.

1140      Review of the long poem Beatrice (Beatriche) by V. Korvin-Piotrovsky in Russia and Slavdom (Rossiya i Slavyanstvo). Paris. October 11, 1930

1141      *Literary Remarks—On Rebellious Angels (Literaturnye zametki—O Vostavshikh Angelakh).* A review of the Prague journal The Will of Russia (Volya Rossii). Nos. 7–8 (1930) in The Rudder (Rul'). Berlin. October 15, 1930. pp. 2–3

1142      *Young Poets (Molodye poèty)* in The Rudder (Rul'). Berlin. January 28, 1931. pp. 2–3
       A review of a book of poems, Black and Azure (Chyornoe i Goluboe), by A. Ladinsky and of an anthology of poems, Crossroads 2 (Perekryostok 2).

1143      Review of a book of poems, Flags (Flagi), by B. Poplavsky in The Rudder (Rul'). Berlin. February 14, 1931. pg. 5

1144      *I. A. Matusevich as Painter (I. A. Matusevich kak khudozhnik)* in The Rudder (Rul'). Berlin. May 6, 1931. pg. 6
       A review of an exhibition of paintings.

1145      *Les écrivains et l'époque* in Le Mois. No. 6. Paris. June–July 1931. pp. 137–142

1146      Review of a novel, The Last and the First (Poslednie i Pervye), by N. Berberova in The Rudder (Rul'). Berlin. July 23, 1931. pg. 5

1147      *What Must Everyone Know? (Chto vsyakij dolzhen znat'?)* in The New Gazette (Novaya Gazeta). No. 5. Paris. 1931
       A satirical article about Freudianism.

1148    *Wolf, Wolf! (Volk, Volk!)* in Our Age (Nash Vek). Berlin. January 31, 1932
        Review of a novel Peace by V. S. Yanovsky.


1149    *In Memory of A. M. Chyorny (Pamyati A. M. Chyornogo)* in The Latest News (Poslednie Novosti). Paris. August 13, 1932


1150    Review of a novel, The Cavern (Peshchera), by M. Aldanov in Contemporary Annals (Sovremennye Zapiski). No. 61. Paris. 1936. pp. 470–472


1151    *Pouchkine ou le vrai et le vraisemblable* in La Nouvelle Revue Française. Volume 48. No. 282. Paris. March 1, 1937. pp. 362–378


1152    A memorial article in In Memory of Amaliya Osipovna Fondaminskaya (Pamyati Amalii Osipovny Fondaminskoi). Paris. Privately printed. 1937. pp. 69–72


1153    *On Khodasevich (O Khodaseviche)* in Contemporary Annals (Sovremennye Zapiski). No. 69. Paris. 1939. pp. 262–265


1154    *Definitions (Opredeleniya)* in The New Russian Word (Novoe Russkoe Slovo). New York. June ?, 1940
        Six short commentaries on political and literary themes.


1155    *Diaghilev and a Disciple.* A review of Serge Diaghilev: An Intimate Biography by Serge Lifar in The New Republic. Washington, D.C. November 18, 1940. pp. 699–700


1156    *Crystal and Ruby.* A review of a translation of The Knight in the Tiger's Skin by Shotha Rostaveli in The New Republic. Washington, D.C. November 25, 1940

1157   *Mr. Masefield and Clio.* A review of Basilissa, a Tale of the Empress Theodora by John Masefield in The New Republic. Washington, D.C. December 9, 1940

1158   *Professor Woodbridge in an Essay on Nature Postulates the Reality of the Word.* A review of An Essay on Nature by Frederick J. E. Woodbridge in The New York Sun. December 10, 1940

1159   Review of the almanac Literary Parade (Literaturnyj Smotr) in Contemporary Annals (Sovremennye Zapiski). No. 70. Paris. Early 1940. pp. 283–285

1160   *Homes for Dukhobors.* A review of Slava Bohu, The Story of the Dukhobors by J. F. C. Wright in The New Republic. Washington, D.C. January 13, 1941. pp. 61–62

1161   *Faint Rose, or the Life of an Artist Who Lived in an Ivory Tower.* A review of The Life and Death of Condor by J. K. Rothenstein in The New York Sun. New York. January 21, 1941

1162   *Mr. Williams' Shakespeare.* A review of Mr. Shakespeare of the Globe by Frayne Williams in The New Republic. Washington, D.C. May 19, 1941. pg. 702

1163   *The Art of Translation* in The New Republic. Washington, D.C. August 4, and September 22, 1941
       For a letter related to this article see *1312.*

1164   *Belloc Essays—Mild But Pleasant.* A review of The Silence of the Sea by Hilaire Belloc in The New York Times Book Review. New York. November 23, 1941

1165   *The Lermontov Mirage* in The Russian Review. Vol. 1. No. 1. November 1941

An essay on the centenary of the poet's death.

Excerpt in Books Abroad. Washington. Spring, 1942

1166    Review of Shakespeare and Democracy by Alwin Thaler and Shakespeare's Audience by Alfred Harbage in The New York Sun. New York. 1941

1167    Review of The Guillotine at Work by G. P. Maximoff in The New York Sun. New York. 1941

1168    *The Creative Writer* in The Bulletin of the New England Modern Languages Association. Boston. January 1942. pp. 21–29

1169    *Lermontov's Dream* in Wellesley Review. Vol. 16. No. 4. Wellesley, Massachusetts. February 1942

1170    *What Faith Means to a Resisting People* in The Wellesley Magazine. Wellesley, Massachusetts. April 1942

1171    *Cabbage Soup and Caviar.* A review of A Treasury of Russian Life and Humor edited by J. Cournos and A Treasury of Russian Literature edited by B. G. Guerney in The New Republic. Washington, D.C. January 17, 1944. pp. 92–93

1172    **NIKOLAI GOGOL.** Norfolk, Connecticut. New Directions. 1944, 1959, 1961. 172pp.

Reprinted: London. Poetry-London. 1947

Reprinted: London. Weidenfeld & Nicolson. 1973

Excerpt (Chapter Five) in Alienation—The Cultural Climate of Modern Man edited by G. Sykes. New York. George Braziller. 1964

Excerpt in Flourish—The Royal Shakespeare Theatre Club Newspaper. No. 5. London.

The date of this publication has not yet been determined.

1173    France: **Nikolai Gogol.** Translated by Marcelle Sibon. Paris. La Table Ronde. 1953

Excerpt entitled "Mort et jeunesse de Gogol" in La Table Ronde. Paris. June 1952

Reprinted: Paris. Union générale d'éditions. 1971

1174    Finland: **Nikolai Gogol.** Translated by Eila Pennanen and Juhani Jaskari. Jyväskylä. K. J. Gummerus. 1963, 1969

1175    Israel: Excerpt in Hasifrut. Tel Aviv. Vol. 1. No. 2. 1968

1176    Italy: **Nicolai Gogol.** Translated by Bruno Oddera. Milan. Mondadori—Il Saggiatore. 1968

1177    *On Learning Russian* in The Wellesley Magazine. Wellesley, Massachusetts. April 1945

1178    *The Place of Russian Studies in the Curriculum* in The Wellesley Magazine. Wellesley, Massachusetts. February 1948

1179    Review of a translation of La Nausée by J. P. Sartre in The New York Times Book Review. New York. April 24, 1949. pp. 3, 19

Excerpt in Nabokov—His Life in Art by A. Field. Boston. Little, Brown. 1967

1180    Introduction to Izbrannoe (Selected Works) by N. Gogol. New York. The Chekhov Publishing House (Izdatel'stvo imeni Chekhova). 1952

1181    *On Translating Pushkin* in Partisan Review. Vol. 22. No. 4. New York. 1955

1182    *Notes of a Translator—I (Zametki perevodchika—I)* in The New Review (Novyj Zhurnal). No. 49. New York. 1957. pp. 130–144

1183    *Notes of a Translator—II (Zametki perevodchika—II)* in Essays (Opyty). No. 8. New York. 1957

1184    Introduction to Lermontov's A Hero of Our Time. New York. Doubleday. 1958
        An introduction to his own translation in collaboration with Dmitri Nabokov.

1185    *The Servile Path* in On Translation edited by Reuben Brower. Cambridge, Massachusetts. Harvard University Press. 1959

1186    Foreword and Commentary to The Song of Igor's Campaign. New York. Vintage Russian Library. 1960. 135pp.
        An introduction and commentary to his own translation.

1187    Review of Walter Arndt's translation of Eugene Onegin in The New York Review of Books. New York. April 30, 1964

1188    Critical Commentary to *Pushkin—Eugene Onegin.* Vol. 2 and 3. Princeton, New Jersey. Bollingen. 1964. 547pp. and 540pp; and London. Routledge & Kegan Paul. 1964
        The translation of Eugene Onegin appears in Vol. 1—see *1303.* A revised translation has been announced. See also *1303.*

1189        *Notes on Prosody.* Princeton, New Jersey. Bollingen. 1964
        One appendix to *Pushkin—Eugene Onegin* published in offprint as limited edition.

1190    *Notes on Prosody.* Princeton, New Jersey. Bollingen. 1965; and London. Routledge & Kegan Paul. 1965
Regular edition, pages renumbered, index added.


1191    *Notes on Prosody and Abram Gannibal.* Princeton, New Jersey. Bollingen. 1969
Two appendices to *Pushkin—Eugene Onegin.*


1192    Notations and Foreword to prison letters of V. D. Nabokov. Aerial Ways (Vozdushnye Puti). No. 4. New York. 1965


1193    *Reply to My Critics* in Encounter. London. February 1966


1194    *'Lolita' and Mr. Girodias* in Evergreen Review. New York. No. 45. February 1967


1195    *On Adaptation* in The New York Review of Books. New York. December 4, 1969. pp. 50–51
An examination of an adaptation by Robert Lowell of a poem by Osip Mandelstam


1196    *Rowe's Symbols.* A review of Nabokov's Deceptive World by William Woodin Rowe in The New York Review of Books. New York. October 7, 1971. pg. 8


1197    *Hommage à Franz Hellens* in Franz Hellens. Brussels. André de Rache. 1971


1197A *Inspiration* in Saturday Review of the Arts. San Francisco. January 1973. pp. 30, 32

Forewords to English works and English translations of Russian works: **Bend Sinister** (Time-Life Books Edition) *0779;* **The Defense** *0667;* **Despair** *0728;* **The Eye** *0695;* **The Gift** *0735;* **Glory** *0726;* **Invitation to a Beheading** *0759;* **Lolita** [Afterword] *0793;* **Nabokov's Quartet** *0878;*

**Poems and Problems** *0353;* **Speak, Memory** [revised] *1096;* **The Waltz Invention** *1072;* **Mary** *0652;* **King, Queen, Knave** *0657;* **A Russian Beauty** *0891*

# Lepidoptera

1198    *A Few Notes on Crimean Lepidoptera* in The Entomologist.
        Vol. 53. London. 1920


1199    *Notes on the Lepidoptera of the Pyrénées Orientales and the
        Ariège* in The Entomologist. Vol. 64. London. 1931


1200    *On Some Asiatic Species of Carterocephalus* in Journal of the
        New York Entomological Society. Vol. 49. New York. 1941


1201    *Lysandra cormion, a New European Butterfly* in Journal of
        the New York Entomological Society. Vol. 49. New York. 1941
        Photographs of types in **Speak, Memory.** *1096*


1202    *Some New or Little-Known Nearctic Neonympha* in Psyche,
        Journal of Entomology. Vol. 49. Cambridge, Massachusetts.
        1942


1203    *The Female of Neonympha maniola Nabokov* in Psyche, Jour-
        nal of Entomology. Vol. 50. Cambridge, Massachusetts. 1943


1204    *The Nearctic Forms of Lycaeides Hüb* in Psyche, Journal of
        Entomology. Vol. 50, Nos. 3–5. Cambridge, Massachusetts.
        1943


1205    *Notes on the Morphology of the Genus Lycaeides* in Psyche,
        Journal of Entomology. Vol. 51. Nos. 3–4. Cambridge, Mas-
        sachusetts. February 1944


1206    *Notes on Neotropical Plebejinae* in Psyche, Journal of Ento-
        mology. Vol. 52. Nos. 1–2. Cambridge, Massachusetts. 1945


1207    *A Third Species of Echinargus Nabokov* in Psyche, Journal
        of Entomology. Vol. 52. Cambridge, Massachusetts. 1945
        Plates.

1208    *A New Species of Cyclargus Nabokov* in The Entomologist. Vol. 81. London. 1948
        Plate


1209    *The Nearctic Members of the Genus Lycaeides Hübner* in Bulletin of the Museum of Comparative Zoology at Harvard College. Vol. 101. Boston. 1949
        Plates.


1210    *Remarks on F. M. Brown's* Measurements and Lepidoptera in The Lepidopterists' News. Vol. 4. New Haven, Connecticut. 1950


1211    *Yesterday's Caterpillar* in The New York Times Book Review. New York. June ?, 1951
        Review of A Field Guide to the Butterflies of North America, East of the Great Plains by A. Klots.


1212    Review of Audubon's Butterflies, Moths and Other Studies edited by A. Ford in The New York Times Book Review. New York. December 28, 1952


1213    *The Female of Lycaeides argyrognomon sublivens Nabokov* in The Lepidopterists' News. Vol. 6. New Haven, Connecticut. 1952. pp. 35–36


1214    *On Some Inaccuracies in Klots'* Field Guide in The Lepidopterists' News. Vol. 6. New Haven, Connecticut. 1952. pg. 41


1215    *Butterfly Collecting in Wyoming* in The Lepidopterists' News. Vol. 7. New Haven, Connecticut. 1953


1216    *Migratory species observed in Wyoming, 1952* in The Lepidopterists' News. Vol. 7. New Haven, Connecticut. 1953

1217   *Comments on Lycaeides argyrognomon in Wisconsin* in The
       Lepidopterists' News. Vol. 7. New Haven, Connecticut. 1953

1218   *Notes on types of Plebejus (Lysandra) cormion Nab.* pg. 288
       of **Speak, Memory.**   *1096*

1219   Review of Collins' A Field Guide to the Butterflies of Britain
       and Europe in Times Educational Supplement. London. Oc-
       tober 23, 1970

# Chess Problems

1220     Chess problem. The Rudder (Rul'). Berlin. May 5, 1923. pg. 5

Chess problems and crossword puzzles by Nabokov appeared sporadically in The Rudder and The Latest News from 1920 to 1940. This is the sole problem which has been located in The Rudder. Several problems in The Latest News follow.

1221     Fairy problem in The Latest News (Poslednie Novosti). Paris. November 17, 1932

This problem was dedicated to E. A. Znosko-Borovsky on his 25th Anniversary. The solution appears November 22, 1932.

Reprinted: The New Statesman. London. December 12, 1969

1222     Problem No. 132 in The Latest News (Poslednie Novosti). Paris. November 25, 1932

1223     Problem No. 134 in The Latest News (Poslednie Novosti). Paris. November 29, 1932

1224     Problem No. 136 in The Latest News (Poslednie Novosti). Paris. December 5, 1932

1225     Chess problem given in the context of memoirs in Partisan Review. No. 3. New York. September 1949

1226     Chess problem in London Evening News. London. October 14, 1967

1227     Chess problems in Sunday Times Magazine. London. November 5, 1967

1228     Chess problem in London Evening News. London. December 24, 1968

1229    Chess problem in The Sunday Times. London. December 29, 1968

1230    Chess problems (Nos. 1004 and C4214) in The Problemist. Volume 8. No. 24. Gloucester, England. November 1969. pg. 398

1231    Chess problem in Trinity Review. Lent. Cambridge. 1969

1232    Chess problems in The Times. London. January 21, 1970

1233    Chess problem (No. C5220) in The Problemist. Volume 9. No. 1. Gloucester, England. January 1970. pg. 6

1234    Chess problem in The Sunday Times. London. February 22, 1970

1235    Chess problems (Nos. 1065 and 1066) in The Problemist. Volume 9. No. 6. Gloucester, England. November 1970. pg. 85

1236    Fourteen chess problems in **Poems and Problems.** 1971  *0353*

1236A  Chess problem (No. 1144) in The Problemist. Volume 9. No. 4. Gloucester, England. March 1972. pg. 201

# Miscellaneous
# Collected
# Reprintings

1237 Four poems in The Anchor (Yakor') edited by Georgy Adamovich and Mikhail Kantor. Berlin. Petropolis. 1936. pp. 194–198
The first comprehensive anthology of Russian émigré poetry.

1238 Five poems in In the West (Na Zapade) edited by Yu. Ivask. New York. Chekhov Publishing House (Izdatel'stvo imeni Chekhova). 1953. pp. 290–298

1239 Four poems in Facets (Grani). Vol. 44. Munich. October–December 1959. pp. 62–63
An anthology issue. See *0303, 0308, 0320, 0323.*

1240 Three poems in A Rhetorical Reader (Chtets-Deklamator) edited by Mart'yanov. New York. 1962. pp. 202, 438–439
An unauthorized reprinting. The editor of this anthology was evidently unaware that Sirin and Nabokov are the same person, because poems are listed under both names.

1241 Seven Russian poems in an Appendix to Nabokov—His Life in Art by Andrew Field. Boston. Little, Brown. 1967. pp. 385–387
See *0076* (one stanza), *0244, 0552,* and excerpts from *0426, 0548, 0601,* and *0609.*

1242 Nabokov's Congeries. Edited by Page Stegner. New York. Viking. 1968
A collection of poetry, prose and criticism including selected passages from the translation of and the commentary on Pushkin's Eugene Onegin. Republished as The Portable Nabokov. New York. Viking. 1971

1243 **Speak, Memory: An Autobiography Revisited**       *1096*
Excerpts

1244 *Terra Incognita*       *0945*

# TRANSLATIONS INTO RUSSIAN

1275    The Sheep (Ovtsy) and Out of the strongs sweetness [sic], two poems by Seumas O'Sullivan in The Rudder (Rul'). Berlin. June 5, 1921. pg. 2

1276    "Quand vous serez bien vieille" ("Kogda na sklone let"). Sonnet by Ronsard (Sonet iz P'era Ronsora) in The Rudder (Rul'). Berlin. August 13, 1922. pg. 2
A poem from Book II of Sonnets pour Hélène.

1277    Colas Breugnon (Nikolka Persik) by Romain Rolland. Berlin. The Word (Slovo). 1922

1278    **Alice in Wonderland (Anya v strane chudes)** by Lewis Carroll. Berlin. Gamayun. 1923. 114pp.

1279    **The Albatross (Albatros)** in The Rudder (Rul'). Berlin. September 3, 1924. pg. 2
A poem by Baudelaire.

1280    The Trick (Podvokh) by X in The Rudder (Rul'). Berlin. September 27, 1925
Translation of an anonymous story in The Manchester Guardian.

1281    Excerpt from In Memoriam by Tennyson in The Link (Zveno). Paris. May 23, 1926

1282    Sonnets XVII and XXVII by Shakespeare in The Rudder (Rul'). Berlin. September 18, 1927

1283    La Nuit de décembre and La Nuit de mai by Alfred de Musset in The Rudder (Rul'). Berlin. October 7, 1928

1284　La Bateau ivre by Arthur Rimbaud in The Rudder (Rul').
　　　　Berlin. December 16, 1928

1285　Excerpts from Hamlet (Act IV, Scene 7; and Act V, Scene
　　　　I) in The Rudder (Rul'). Berlin. October 19, 1930

1286　Hamlet's monologue (Act III, Scene I) in The Rudder (Rul').
　　　　Berlin. November 23, 1930

1287　Prologue to Goethe's Faust in The Latest News (Poslednie
　　　　Novosti). Paris. December 15, 1932
　　　　　Another source has offered a different date, December
　　　　12, 1933, for the appearance of this translation.

1288　Poems by Rupert Brooke.
　　　　　These translations occur within the context of Nabokov's
　　　　article on Brooke. See *1108*.

1289　Poems by Verlaine, Supervielle, and Yeats.
　　　　　Unlocated. These translations, which Nabokov recalled
　　　　in the Rowohlt bibliography having published, do not
　　　　occur in Nabokov's early poetic notebooks which in all
　　　　other respects are quite inclusive in regard to his early
　　　　art.

1290　Poems by Byron and Keats in **The Empyrean Path.**　*0086*

1291　Gettysburg Address in Lincoln's Gettysburg Address in Transla-
　　　　tion compiled by Roy P. Basler. Library of Congress.
　　　　Washington. 1972

## TRANSLATIONS INTO FRENCH

1292　*Vers composés pendant l'insomnie* in Hommage à Pouchkine
　　　　1837–1937, edited by Zinaida Schakhowskoy. Brussels. Les
　　　　Cahiers du journal des poètes. No. 28. February 5, 1937

1293  Four poems by Pushkin incorporated in an essay in La Nouvelle Revue Française. Vol. 48. No. 282. Paris. March 1, 1937

## TRANSLATIONS INTO ENGLISH

1294  **Mozart and Salieri** by Pushkin in The New Republic. Washington, D.C. April 21, 1942
Translated in collaboration with Edmund Wilson.


1295  *Alter Ego, "When life is torture . . .",* and *The Swallow* by Afanasi Fet in The Russian Review. Vol. 3, No. 1. Hanover, New Hampshire. Autumn 1943


1296  The Monkey, Poem and Orpheus by Vladislav Khodasevich in New Directions in Prose and Poetry edited by James Laughlin. Norfolk, Connecticut. New Directions. 1941. pp. 597–600.


1296A  "What is the use of time and rhyme" and Stanzas by Vladislav Khodasevich in A Second Book of Russian Verse edited by C. M. Bowra. London. Macmillan. 1948. pg. 91
"What is the use of time and rhyme" is the first line of Poem which is listed in New Directions Anthology. These poems have been reprinted in a special issue of Tri-Quarterly (No. 26) devoted to Russian émigré literature.


1297  **THREE RUSSIAN POETS: TRANSLATIONS OF PUSHKIN, LERMONTOV, AND TYUTCHEV.** Norfolk, Connecticut. New Directions. 1944; and London. Lindsay Drummond. 1947


1298  Poems of Fyodor Ivanovich Tyutchev in The Atlantic Monthly. January 1944

Reprinted: Four lines of Tyutchev's *Silentium* in *Russian Intellectual History* by Gertrude Vakar. New York. Harcourt, Brace. 1965

*1299*    Excerpts from Eugene Onegin in The Russian Review. Vol. 4, No. 2. Hanover, New Hampshire. Spring 1945
Rhymed translations of three stanzas.

*1300*    Thanksgiving by Mikhail Lermontov in The Atlantic Monthly. November 1946

*1301*    **A Hero of Our Time** by Mikhail Lermontov. New York. Doubleday. 1958
Translated in collaboration with Dmitri Nabokov. Includes introduction, commentary and map.

*1302*    **The Song of Igor's Campaign.** Anonymous. New York. Vintage. 1960; and London. Weidenfeld & Nicolson. 1960
A translation and commentary.

Excerpts in The Penguin Book of Modern Verse Translation edited by G. Steiner. Harmondsworth. Penguin. 1968

*1303*    **Pushkin—Eugene Onegin.** Four volumes. Princeton, N.J. Bollingen. 1964; and London. Routledge & Kegan Paul. 1964
A new Bollingen edition containing a revised translation and commentaries will appear.

Nabokov's own works translated either by Nabokov himself or in collaboration with others.

*0353 0706*
*0651 0726*
*0657 0728*
*0667 0735*
*0695 0759*
*0726 0794*
*0891*

# Letters and Interviews

1304    Letter in The Russian Gazette (Russkaya Gazeta). Berlin. August 26, 1923?

1305    Autour de Maiakovsky. A collective letter on the death of Mayakovsky in Les Nouvelles littéraires. Paris. July 12, 1930 N. B. Nabokov's name was added to the list of signatories through a misunderstanding.

1306    Reply to a questionnaire "Enquête internationale sur le populisme" in La Grande Revue. Paris. December 1930

1307    Reply to a questionnaire on Proust in Numbers (Chisla). No. 1. Paris. 1930. pg. 274

       English: Translated by A. Field in Nabokov—His Life in Art. Boston. Little, Brown. 1967. pg. 265

1308    "A Meeting with V. Sirin" ("Vstrecha s V. Sirinym") by Andrei Sedykh in Today (Segodnya). Riga. November 4, 1932

1309    Letter in The Latest News (Poslednie Novosti). Paris. 1937? The precise date has not been established.

1310    Anniversary salutation in Border (Rubezh). No. 14. Kharbin. 1938

1311    Letter in The New Russian Word (Novoe Russkoe Slovo). New York. April 9, 1941

1312    Letter in The New Republic. Washington, D.C. December 22, 1941
       Reply to a letter correcting **The Art of Translation.**

1313    Interview in Wellesley College News. Wellesley, Massachusetts. 1941

1314    "From V. Nabokov-Sirin" ("Ot V. Nabokova-Sirina"). The New Russian Word (Novoe Russkoe Slovo). November 4, 1956
On the death of Mark Aldanov.

1315    Interview in New York Post. New York. August 6, 1958

1316    Letter in The Cornell Sun. Ithaca, New York. October 20, 1958

1317    Interview in Newsweek. New York. November 24, 1958

1318    Interview in Louisville Courier-Journal. Louisville, Kentucky. January 25, 1959

1319    Letter in Life. New York. July 6, 1959

1320    Interview conducted together with Alain Robbe-Grillet in Arts. Paris. No. 746. October 28–November 3, 1959

1321    "A Conversation with Vladimir Nabokov" by J. G. Hayman in Twentieth Century. London. December 1959

1322    Interview with Helen Lawrenson in Esquire. New York. August 1960
Subsequent corrections and cartoon published September 1960

1323    Interview in Epoch. Los Angeles. 1960

1324    "A Meeting with the Author of *Lolita*" by Gershon Svet in Russian Thought (Russkaya Mysl'). Paris. February 7, 1961;

and New Russian Word (Novoe Russkoe Slovo). New York. February ?, 1961

1325    Interview in Nice-Matin. Nice. April 3, 1961

1326    Letter in Esquire. New York. June 1961

1327    Letter in Playboy. Chicago. July 1961

1328    Letter in The Times. London. May 30, 1962

1329    Interview with Phyllis Meras in New York Herald-Tribune. New York. June 1, 1962

1330    Interview in Saturday Review. New York. June 12, 1962

1331    Interview in Victoria Colonist. British Columbia. July 15, 1962

1332    Cancelled.

1333    Letter in Encounter. London. September 1962. pg. 94

1334    "Vladimir Nabokov on His Life and Work." Interview with P. D. Smith in The Listener. London. November 22, 1962. pp. 856–858

1335    Interview in Tribune de Lausanne. Lausanne. September 1, 1963

1336    Letter in Russian Thought (Russkaya Mysl'). Paris. October 8, 1963

1337    Interview with Alvin Toffler in Playboy. Chicago. January 1964

Included in Playboy Interviews. Chicago. Playboy Press. 1964; and The Twelfth Anniversary Playboy Reader. Chicago. Playboy Press. 1965

1338    Interview remarks in article on Nabokov in Life. New York. November 20, 1964

1339    Letter in New Statesman. London. January 22, 1965. pg. 112

1340    Letter in New Statesman. London. April 23, 1965. pg. 642

1341    Letter in The New York Review of Books. New York. August 26, 1965

1342    Reply to questionnaire in The New York Times. New York. September 1, 1965

1343    Letter in The New York Review of Books. January 20, 1966

1344    Interview in The New York Times. New York. January 30, 1966. pg. 17
Excerpts from a National Educational Television interview directed by Robert Hughes.

1345    Letter in Encounter. London. February 1966

1346    Letter in Encounter. London. April 1966

1347    Letter in Encounter. London. May 1966

*1348*   Interview in Die Zeit. Hamburg. November 1, 1966

*1349*   Interview with Penelope Gilliatt in Vogue. New York. December 1966

*1350*   Letter in The Sunday Times. London. January 1, 1967

*1351*   Interview in Saturday Evening Post. Philadelphia. February 18, 1967

*1352*   Letter in Encounter. London. February 1967

*1353*   Letter in Evergreen Review. New York. February 1967

*1354*   Two letters in Saturday Evening Post. Philadelphia. March 25, 1967

*1355*   Letter in Playboy. Chicago. May 1967

*1356*   Interview with Drago Arsenijevic in La Tribune (Supplement of Tribune de Genève). Geneva. October 25, 1967

*1357*   Interview with Herbert Gold in The Paris Review. Paris. October 1967

*1358*   Letter in New Statesman. London. November 17, 1967. pg. 680

*1359*   Interview with Pierre Dommergues in Le Monde. Paris. November 22, 1967

1360    Interview with Alfred Appel, Jr. in Wisconsin Studies in Contemporary Literature. Vol. 8. No. 2. Madison, Wisconsin. Spring 1967
        Included in Nabokov—The Man and His Work edited by L. S. Dembo. Madison, Wisconsin. University of Wisconsin Press. 1968

1361    Interview with Pat Garian in Harper's Bazaar (German edition). 1967

1362    Letter in New Statesman. London. January 19, 1968. pg. 78

1363    Interview with Martin Esslin in New York Times Book Review. New York. May 12, 1968. pg. 4; 50–51

1364    "The Strong Opinions of Vladimir Nabokov." Interview with Nicolas Garnham in The Listener. London. October 10, 1968. pp. 463–464

1365    *Nabokov on Nabokov and Things.* New York Times Book Review. December 5, 1968

1366    "La Nouvelle Lolita de Nabokov" in Match de Paris. Paris. January 11, 1969
        N.B. A bogus interview.

1367    Interview with Alden Whitman in The New York Times. New York. April 19, 1969. pg. 20

1368    Interview with Martha Duffy in Time. New York. May 23, 1969. pp. 43–48

1369    Interview with Philip Oakes in The Sunday Times. London. June 1969

1370   "'To be kind, to be proud, to be fearless'". Interview with
       James Mossman in The Listener. London. October 23, 1969.
       pp. 560–561
       Reprinted in Soma. No. 18–19. Amsterdam. November–
          December 1971


1371   Interview with Claudio Gorlier in Corriere della Sera. October
       30, 1969


1372   Interview with Nantas Salvalaggio in Il Giorno. Rome. No-
       vember 3, 1969


1373   Interview with Allene Talmey in Vogue. New York. Decem-
       ber 1969


1374   Interview with Gaetano Tumiati in La Stampa. Torino. 1969


1375   Interview with Marina Bulgherini in American Literature.
       Catania. 1969


1376   Interview with Costanzo Costantini in Il Messaggero. 1969


1377   Interview with Roberto Tabozzi in Panorama. Rome. 1969?


1378   Interview with Nurit Beretzky in Ma'Ariv. Tel Aviv. Israel.
       February 13, 1970


1378   Reply to questionnaire in The Sea (Umi). Vol. 1. No. 1. Tokyo.
       June 1970
          This reply, given by Mrs. Nabokov for her husband,
          appears in English.


1379   Interview with Hanspeter Riklin for Swiss newspapers. 1970

There is no record by title of the Swiss newspaper in which this interview appeared.

1380   "Anniversary Notes" in Supplement to Tri-Quarterly 17. Evanston, Illinois. 1970. 15pp.

1381   Excerpt from a private letter in the Editor's Foreword to The Provisional Government by V. D. Nabokov. Brisbane. University of Queensland Press. 1970. pg. vi

1382   Interview compiled and translated by L. Dušková in Světová Literaturá. No. 4. Prague
       N. B. A bogus interview composed of excerpts from the introduction to the English version of **The Defense** and the Russian version of **Lolita,** from previous interviews in Le Monde and L'Express, and from **Other Shores.**

1383   Letter in Time. New York. January 18, 1971. pg. 2

1384   Letter in Time. New York. July 5, 1971. pg. 2

1385   Letter in New York Times Book Review. New York. November 7, 1971
       An exchange with Edmund Wilson over biographical inaccuracies in Wilson's Upstate.

1386   Interview with Israel Shenker in New York Times Book Review. New York. January 9, 1972. pg. 2

1387   Letter in Playboy. Chicago. January 1972. pg. 18
       Illustrated with a drawing.

1388   Letter in New York Times Book Review. New York. March 5, 1972

# Epigrams and Casual Items

1389    Cancelled.


1390    *"Historical Anecdotes* [From Old Calendars]" (*"Istoricheskie
        anekdoty* [Iz starykh kalendarej]"); *"Friends, Russian
        Strongmen, An Eccentric"* (*"Druz'ya; Russkie silachi;
        Original"*) in The Rudder (Rul'). Berlin. December 25, 1929
            Fillers in the section of The Rudder called "Tarantas No.
        1," said to be "Contributed by Professor Strufionov."


1391    *"From the Newspapers"* (*"Iz gazet"*) in The Rudder (Rul').
        Berlin. January 19, 1930
            Invented journalistic absurdities in the section of The
        Rudder called "Tarantas No. 2."


1392    (*Untitled*) in The Latest News (Poslednie Novosti). Paris. Jan-
        uary 2, 1932
            Brief charity appeal in regard to the desperate position
        of the unemployed.


1393    *"Remembrance: Unreal Estate,"* an aphorism in Reader's
        Digest. Pleasantville, New York. 1966
            Taken from **Speak, Memory.**


1394    *"No greater crook"* (*"Takogo net moshennika vtorogo"*)
            An epigram at the expense of the émigré poet Georgy
        Ivanov, published for the first time in Nabokov—His Life
        in Art by A. Field. Boston. Little, Brown. 1967. pg. 379

# Émigré Reviews
# of Nabokov

After this manuscript had gone to the printer, a descriptive article entitled "Nabokov in Russian Émigré Criticism," by Professor Ludmila Foster (**Russian Literature Tri-Quarterly,** No. 3, 1972), reached me. Though the article is more circumscribed in scope than the bibliography which follows (Professor Foster lists only articles which appeared in journals), there are a few additions to my own listing. These have been appended in the Addenda as has the first bibliographical information about a heretofore unknown long article devoted mainly to the later Sirin works by Dr. N. Andreyev, the author of the first serious study, in 1930 (cf. 1465), of the early Sirin works.

1395    Review of **The Cluster** and **The Empyrean Path** by P.Sh. in The Rudder (Rul'). Berlin. January 28, 1923

1396    Review of **The Cluster** by G. Rosimov (Yu. Ofrosimov) in The New Russian Book (Novaya Russkaya Kniga). Berlin. May–June 1923. pg. 23

1397    Review of **The Cluster** by G (Roman Gul') in The New Russian Book (Novaya Russkaya Kniga). Berlin. 1923

1398    Review of **The Empyrean Path** by V. Lur'e in The New Russian Book (Novaya Russkaya Kniga). Berlin. 1923

1399    Article on **The Tragedy of Mister Morn** by E. K-n. in The Rudder (Rul'). Berlin. April 6, 1924. pg. 8

1400    Report of ballet The Gentleman of the Moonlight (Kavaler lunnogo sveta) as performed in Königsberg in The Rudder (Rul'). Berlin. March ?, 1925
Nabokov wrote a two-page scenario for this ballet in collaboration with Ivan Lukash. It has never been published.

1401    Review of *La Bonne Lorraine* by Yu. Aikhenval'd in The Rudder (Rul'). Berlin. May 13, 1925

1402    "Literary notes" ("Literaturnye zametki") by Yu. Aikhenval'd in The Rudder (Rul'). Berlin. March 31, 1926
Review of **Mary.**

1403    Review of **Mary** by Gleb Struve in Renaissance (Vozrozhdenie). Paris. April 1, 1926

1404    Review of **Mary** by S. Korev in The Word (Slovo). Riga. April 9, 1926

1405    "Dream and Impotence" ("Mechta i bessil'e") by A. S. Izgoev
in The Rudder (Rul'). Berlin. April 14, 1926
Review of **Mary.**


1406    "A Novel by V. Sirin" ("Roman V. Sirina") by K. Mochul'sky
in The Link (Zveno). No. 168. Paris. April 18, 1926
Review of **Mary.**


1407    Review of **Mary** by A. Savel'ev in The Latest News (Poslednie
Novosti). No. 1963. Paris. April 22, 1926


1408    Review of **Mary** by Yu. Aikhenval'd in The Russian Word
(Russkoe Slovo). Kharbin. May 22, 1926
A reprint of the review which appeared in The Rudder.


1409    Review of **Mary** by Mikhail Osorgin in Contemporary Annals
(Sovremennye Zapiski). No. 28. Paris. 1926. pp. 474–476


1410    Review of **Mary** by Ars. M. (A. Damanskaja) in Days (Dni).
No. 1159. Paris. 1926


1411    Review of **Mary** by Nadezhda Mel'nikova-Papoushkova in The
Will of Russia (Volya Rossii). Vol. 5. Prague. 1926. pp. 196–98


1412    Review of **Mary** by "A" (Prince D. A. Shakovsky, now Arch-
bishop Ioann of San Francisco) in The Well-Intentioned
(Blagonamerennyj). Brussels. 1926


1413    Review of *Terror* by Mikhail Osorgin in The Latest News
(Poslednie Novosti). Paris. January 27, 1927


1414    "Literary notes" ("Literaturnye zametki") by Yu.
Aikhenval'd on *Terror* in The Rudder (Rul'). Berlin. February 2, 1927

1415    Review of *Terror* by Diks in The Link (Zveno). Paris. February 13, 1927

1416    Review of **The Man from the USSR** by Boris Brodsky and V. Iretssky in The Rudder (Rul'). Berlin. April 5, 1927
        Although this two-part review is signed by Brodsky alone the first section is by Iretssky.

1417    Review of *A University Poem* by Gleb Struve in Russia (Rossiya). Paris. December 10, 1927

1418    Review of **Mary** in The Will of Russia (Volya Rossii). No. 5–6. Prague. 1927
        There is another 1927 listing for an article in this journal entitled "Young Émigré Literature" by S. Postnikov in which **Mary** and some short stories are discussed. It may be the same article but unfortunately this cannot be checked as this manuscript goes to press.

1419    "Literary notes" ("Literaturnye zametki") by Yu. Aikhenval'd on *A University Poem* in The Rudder (Rul'). Berlin. January 4, 1928

1420    Review of **King, Queen, Knave** by Gleb Struve in Russia (Rossiya). No. 1. Paris. January 12, 1928

1421    Review of **King, Queen, Knave** by Yu. Aikhenval'd in The Rudder (Rul'). Berlin. August 3, 1928

1422    Review of **King, Queen, Knave** in The Latest News (Poslednie Novosti). Paris. August 4, 1928

1423    *Review of* **King, Queen, Knave** by Gleb Struve in Russia and Slavdom (Rossiya i Slavyanstvo). No. 1. Paris. December 1, 1928

1424    Review of **King, Queen, Knave** by Mikhail Tsetlin in Contemporary Annals (Sovremennye Zapiski). Paris. No. 37. 1928. pp. 536–39

1425    Review of **Mary** and **King, Queen, Knave** in Ost-Europa. Berlin. January 4, 1929
        In German.

1426    "Literature in Exile" ("Literatura v izgnanii") by Aleksandr Amfiteatrov in The New Time (Novoe Vremya). Belgrade. May 22–23, 1929
        An article in two parts with significant reference to **Mary** and **King, Queen, Knave.**

1427    Review of **The Defense** by Georgy Adamovich in The Latest News (Poslednie Novosti). Paris. October 21, 1929

1428    Review of **The Defense** by Pyotr Pil'sky in Today (Segodnya). Riga. October 22, 1929
        There is a conflicting date of October 10 for this review, and a library holding these dates has not yet been located.

1429    Review of **The Defense** by Vladislav Khodasevich in Renaissance (Vozrozhdenie). Paris. October 24, 1929

1430    "The World of Bunin and the World of Sirin" ("Buninskij mir i Sirinskij mir") by K. Zajtsev in Russia and Slavdom (Rossiya i Slavyanstvo). Paris. November 9, 1929
        With special reference to **The Defense.**

1431    Review of **The Defense** by A. Savel'ev in The Rudder (Rul'). Berlin. November 20, 1929

1432    Review of **The Defense** by Georgy Adamovich in Illustrated Russia (Illustrirovannaya Rossiya). Berlin. December 7, 1929

1433    "New Russian Books" ("Russkie Novinki") by A. Savel'ev (S. Sherman) in The Rudder (Rul'). Berlin. December 31, 1929
On **The Return of Chorb.**

1434    Review of **The Return of Chorb** by Pyotr Pil'sky in Today (Segodnya). Riga. January 12, 1930

1435    Review of **The Defense** by Pyotr Pil'sky in Today (Segodnya). Riga. January 29, 1930

1436    Review of **The Defense** by Georgy Adamovich in The Latest News (Poslednie Novosti). Paris. February 13, 1930

1437    Review of **The Defense** and **King, Queen, Knave** by André Levinson in Les Nouvelles Littéraires. No. 383. Paris. February 15, 1930
In French.

1438    Review of **The Defense** by A. Savel'ev in The Rudder (Rul'). Berlin. February 19, 1930

1439    Article by Vladislav Khodasevich in Renaissance (Vozrozhdenie). Paris. March 3, 1930

1440    "Remarks about Poetry" ("Zametki o Stikhakh") by Gleb Struve in Russia and Slavdom (Rossiya i Slavyanstvo). Paris. March 16, 1930
On Sirin and other émigré poets.

1441    Review of **The Return of Chorb** by G. Kh. (German Khokhlov) in The Will of Russia (Volya Rossii). Prague. No. 2. March 1930. pp. 190–92

1442    "Literary Customs" ("Literaturnye Nravy") in The Rudder (Rul'). Berlin. April 4, 1930

Unsigned. On G. Ivanov's essay in Numbers.

1443   Comment by Kirill Zajtsev in Russia and Slavdom (Rossiya i Slavyanstvo). Paris. April 5, 1930
On G. Ivanov's essay in Numbers.

1444   "Remarks about Poetry" ("Zametki o stikhakh") by Gleb Struve in Russia and Slavdom (Rossiya i Slavyanstvo). Paris. April ?, 1930
A review of the poems in **The Return of Chorb.**

1445   Comment by Marc Slonim in The Will of Russia (Volya Rossii). No. 3. Prague. April 1930
On G. Ivanov's essay in Numbers.

1446   Review of **The Defense** by Pyotr Pil'sky in Today (Segodnya). Riga. May 10, 1930

1447   "Russian Literature in Emigration" ("Russkaya literatura v èmigratsii") by Vladimir Weidle in Renaissance (Vozrozhdenie). Paris. May 12, 1930
On **The Defense.**

1448   Review of **The Defense** by Georgy Adamovich in The Latest News (Poslednie Novosti). Paris. May 15, 1930

1449   "The Art of Sirin" ("Tvorchestvo Sirina") by Gleb Struve in Russia and Slavdom (Rossiya i Slavyanstvo). Paris. May 17, 1930

1450   Review of **The Defense** by A. Savel'ev in The Rudder (Rul'). Berlin. May 21, 1930

1451   "Russian Literature in Emigration" ("Russkaya literatura v
       èmigratsii") by Vladislav Khodasevich in Renaissance
       (Vozrozhdenie). Paris. June 19, 1930
       On **The Defense.**


1452   "Russian Literature in Emigration" ("Russkaya literatura v
       èmigratsii") by Vladimir Weidle in Renaissance
       (Vozrozhdenie). Paris. July 24, 1930
       Review of *Pilgram.*


1453   Review of **The Defense** by Nikolaj Federof in **News** (Novosti).
       Zagreb. July 27, 1930
       In Serbian.


1454   Review of *Pilgram* by Pyotr Pil'sky in Today (Segodnya).
       Riga. July 1930


1455   Review of *Pilgram* by Georgy Adamovich in The Latest News
       (Poslednie Novosti). Paris. August 7, 1930


1456   Review of *Pilgram* by A. Savel'ev in The Rudder (Rul'). Ber-
       lin. August 15, 1930


1457   Review of **The Defense** by M. O. in The New Russian Word
       (Novoe Russkoe Slovo). New York. August ?, 1930


1458   Review of **The Return of Chorb** by S. Nal'yanch in For Free-
       dom (Za svobodu). No. 209. Warsaw. August ?, 1930


1459   Review of *Pilgram* by Lolly L'vov in Russia and Slavdom
       (Rossiya i Slavyanstvo). Paris. September 6, 1930


1460   Review of **The Defense** by Georgy Adamovich in Illustrated
       Russia (Illyustrirovannaya Rossiya). No. 42. October 4, 1930

1461    Review of **The Defense** (separate edition) by Vladislav Khodasevich in Renaissance (Vozrozhdenie). Paris. October 11, 1930

1462    Review of **The Eye** by Vladimir Weidle in Renaissance (Vozrozhdenie). Paris. October 30, 1930

1463    Review of **The Defense** by A. Savel'ev in The Rudder (Rul'). No. 2994. Berlin. October ?, 1930

1464    Review of **The Defense** by M. B. in The New Russian Word (Novoe Russkoe Slovo). New York. October 1930

1465    "Sirin" by Nikolay Andreyev in Virgin Soil (Nov'). No. 3. Tallin, Estonia. October 1930
        A survey article. Translated in The Complection of Russian Literature. London. Allen Lane. 1971. Pelican. 1973

1466    Review of **The Eye** by Kirill Zajtsev in Russia and Slavdom (Rossiya i Slavyanstvo). Paris. November 15, 1930

1467    Review of **The Eye** by Georgy Adamovich in The Latest News (Poslednie Novosti). Paris. November 27, 1930

1468    Review of **The Eye** by Pyotr Pil'sky in Today (Segodnya). Riga. November ?, 1930

1469    Review of **The Eye** by Sergej Yablonovsky in The Rudder (Rul'). Berlin. December 6, 1930

1470    Review of **The Defense** by Arthur Luther in Ost-Europa. Berlin. December 1930
        In German.

*1471*   Review of **Mary, King, Queen, Knave, The Defense,** and **The Return of Chorb** by Georgy Ivanov in Numbers (Chisla). No. 1. Paris. 1930. pp. 233–236
    This ad hominem attack gave rise to a number of articles and comments in the Russian émigré press.


*1472*   Review of **The Return of Chorb** by Mikhail Tsetlin in Contemporary Annals (Sovremennye Zapiski). Paris. No. 42. 1930. pp. 530–531


*1473*   Comment by Anton Krainy in Numbers (Chisla). Nos. 2–3. Paris. 1930
    On G. Ivanov's review in the previous issue of **Numbers.** Anton Krainy was a pseudonym of Zinaida Gippius.


*1474*   Review of **The Defense** by Al. Novik (G. Khokhlov) in Contemporary Annals (Sovremennye Zapiski). No. 45. Paris. 1930. pp. 514–517


*1475*   Review of **Glory** by A. Savel'ev in The Rudder (Rul'). Berlin. February 25, 1931


*1476*   Review of **Glory** by Vladimir Weidle in Renaissance (Vozrozhdenie). Paris. February 26, 1931


*1477*   Review of **Glory** by Pyotr Pil'sky in Today (Segodnya). Riga. February ?, 1931


*1478*   Review of **Glory** by Yu. Sazonov (Yuliya Sazonova-Slonimskaya) in The Latest News (Poslednie Novosti). Paris. March 3, 1931


*1479*   Review of **Glory** by Kirill Zajtsev in The Latest News (Poslednie Novosti). Paris. March 5, 1931

Bezdumnyj Kritik") by V. Anichkov in New Dawn (Novaya Zarya). New York. April ?, 1934

1500 "Books and People" ("Knigi i lyudi") by Vladislav Khodasevich in Renaissance (Vozrozhdenie). Paris. May 3, 1934
A review of **Despair** on its appearance in Contemporary Annals.

1501 Review of **Despair** by Georgy Adamovich in The Latest News (Poslednie Novosti). Paris. May 24, 1934

1502 "V. V. Sirin—A New Star in Literature" ("V. V. Sirin—Novaya Zvezda v Literature") in New Dawn (Novaya Zarya). New York. August 11, 1934

1503 Article on Sirin by Zinaida Shakhovskaya in Le Thyrse— Revue d'Art et de Littérature. Brussels. September 1, 1934
In French.

1504 Article in The New Word (Novoe Slovo). No. 12. Berlin. November 1934
An account of a panel discussion of Sirin's art that was held in Kharbin, Manchuria.

1505 "Sirin" by A. Isačenko in Annals of Literature and Criticism (Listy pro umeni a kritiku). No. 13–14. Prague. 1934
In Czech.

1506 Review of **Camera obscura** by Yu. Terapiano in Numbers (Chisla). No. 10. Paris. 1934. pp. 287–288

1507 Review of **Camera obscura** by Mikhail Osorgin in Contemporary Annals (Sovremennye Zapiski). Vol. 54. Paris. 1934. pp. 458–460

1508    "Books and People" ("Knigi i lyudi") by Vladislav Khodasevich in Renaissance (Vozrozhdenie). Paris. July 11, 1935
Review of **Invitation to a Beheading.**

1509    Review of **Invitation to a Beheading** by Pyotr Pil'sky in Today
(Segodnya). Riga. July 1935

1510    "The Pride of Émigré Literature—V. Sirin" ("Gordost'
èmigrantskoj literatury—V. Sirin) by Nataliya Reznikova
in Dawn (Zarya). Kharbin. October 27, 1935

1511    "A Suffocating World" ("Dushnyj mir") by Vladimir
Kadashev in The New Word (Novoe Slovo). Berlin. March
27, 1936
A survey article on Sirin's prose.

1512    "About V. Sirin" ("O V. Sirine") by Gleb Struve in The Russian in England (Russkij v Anglii). London. May 15, 1936

1513    Review of **Despair** by Vladimir Weidle in The Circle (Krug).
No. 1. Paris. 1936. pp. 185–187

1514    Review of **Despair** by Gleb Struve in The Russian in England
(Russkij v Anglii). No. 9. London. 1936

1515    "The Rebirth of Allegory" ("Vozrozhdenie allegorii") by
Pyotr Bitsilli in Contemporary Annals (Sovremennye
Zapiski). Vol. 61. Paris. 1936. pp. 191–204
An essay comparing Nabokov with Saltykov-Shchedrin.

1516    "Vladimir Sirin-Nabokov—A prelude to his evening in London on February 20" ("Vladimir Sirin-Nabokov—k ego
vecheru v Londone 20-ogo fevralya") by Gleb Struve in The
Russian in England (Russkij v Anglii). London. February 16,
1937

1517    "'On Sirin' in 'Books and People'" ("'O Sirine' in 'Knigi i lyudi'") by Vladislav Khodasevich in Renaissance (Vozrozhdenie). Paris. February ?, 1937

1518    Review of **The Eye** by S. Savel'ev (Savely Sherman) in Russian Annals (Russkie Zapiski). No. 10. Paris. 1938. pp. 195–97

1519    "Sirin's **The Event** in the Russian Theatre (**Sobytie** Sirina v Russkom Teatre) by Vladislav Khodasevich in Contemporary Annals (Sovremennye Zapiski). Vol. 66. Paris. 1938. pp. 423–27

1520    "In regard to V. Sirin's **The Event**" ("Po povodu **Sobytiya** V. Sirina") by Lidiya Chervinskaya in The Circle (Krug). No. 3. Paris. 1938. pp. 168–70

1521    Essay on **Invitation to a Beheading** and **The Eye** by Pyotr Bitsilli in Contemporary Annals (Sovremennye Zapiski). Vol. 68. 1939. pp. 474–77

1522    Review of **Invitation to a Beheading** by Sergei Osokin in Russian Annals (Russkie Zapiski). No. 13. Paris. 1939. pp. 198–99

1523    Review of **Nikolai Gogol** by Georgy Fedotov in The New Review (Novyj Zhurnal). Vol. 9. New York. 1944. pp. 368–70

1524    "A Meeting with the Poet" ("Vstrecha s poètom") an interview-article by G. Aronson in The New Russian Word (Novoe Russkoe Slovo). New York. May 26, 1949

1525    "On a Fashionable Writer" ("O modnom pisatele") by G. I. Yasinitsky in Russian Life (Russkaya Zhizn'). U.S.A? September 17, 1949

*1526*    Review of **Poems** (1952) by A. Nejmirok in Borders (Grani). Vol. 16. 1952. pp. 179–81

*1527*    Review of **Poems** (1952) by Yurij Ivask in Essays (Opyty).No. 1. New York. 1953. pp. 194–99

*1528*    "On Sirin" ("O Sirine") in Literary Articles and Recollections by Vladislav Khodasevich. The Chekhov Publishing House (Izdatel'stvo imeni Chekhova). New York. 1954

*1529*    "Vladimir Nabokov" in Solitude and Freedom (Odinochestvo i Svoboda) by Georgy Adamovich. New York. The Chekhov Publishing House (Izdatel'stvo imeni Chekhova). 1955
A chapter devoted to Nabokov.

*1530*    Review of **Poems** (1952) by Ekaterina Tauber in Renaissance (Vozrozhdenie). Vol. 37. Paris. 1955. pp. 139–41

*1531*    "On Poplavsky and Nabokov" ("O Poplavskom i Nabokove") by Vladimir Varshavsky in Essays (Opyty). No. 4. New York. 1955. pp. 65–72

*1532*    Review of **Other Shores** by Nikita Majer in Renaissance (Vozrozhdenie). Vol. 39. Paris. 1955

*1533*    A chapter on **Invitation to a Beheading** in The Unnoticed Generation (Nezamechyonnoe Pokolenie) by Vladimir Varshavsky. The Chekhov Publishing House (Izdatel'stvo imeni Chekhova). New York. 1956

*1533A*  A survey of Nabokov's poetry and prose in Russian Literature in Exile (Russkaya literatura v izgnanii) by Gleb Struve. The Chekhov Publishing House (Izdatel'stvo imeni Chekhova). New York. 1956.
A discussion in two sections. In the first Nabokov's Russian poetry is dismissed as weak and derivative; in the

second, there is a presentation of excerpts from émigré criticism of Nabokov's prose.

1534  Review of **Spring in Fialta** by A. K. (Aleksandr Kashin) in Facets (Grani). Vol. 33. 1957. pp. 222–24

1535  "Lolita and The Splitting of the Atom" ("Lolita i Raspad Atoma") by Vladimir Zlobin in Renaissance (Vozrozhdenie). Vol. 85. Paris. 1959. pp. 133–39
A comparison of Nabokov and Georgy Ivanov.

1536  "The Fate of Passion" ("Uchast' strasti") by Nikolaj Armazov in Facets (Grani). Vol. 42. 1959. pp. 231–36
A review of **Lolita.**

1537  "Nabokov and his Lolita" ("Nabokov i ego Lolita") by Nina Berberova in The New Review (Novyj Zhurnal). Vol. 57. New York. 1959. pp. 92–115

1538  "On the Particular Features and Basic Stages in the Development of Russian Literature Abroad" ("Ob osobennostyakh i : osnovnykh ètapakh razvitiya russkoj literatury za rubezhom") by N. Andreyev in Russian Literature Abroad—a collection of essays (Russkaya literatura v èmigratsii—sbornik statej), edited by N. Poltoratsky. University of Pittsburgh Press. Pittsburgh. 1972. pp. 15-39
A survey article with particular attention devoted to Nabokov.

1539  "The Most Recent Book of V. Nabokov" ("Poslednyaya kniga V. Nabokova") by Marc Slonim in Russian Thought (Russkaya Mysl'). Paris. March 8, 1973.
On Transparent Things.

# Russian Émigré Journals
# —An Appendix

Aerial Ways (Vozdushnye Puti)
A series of five literary almanacs edited and published by Roman Grynberg in New York between 1960 and 1967.


Circle, The (Krug)
A series of four literary almanacs which first began to appear in Paris in 1936.


Contemporary Annals (Sovremennye Zapiski)
The foremost publication of the Russian emigration, originally a monthly, then a quarterly, published in Paris between 1920 and 1940 and edited by I. Fondaminsky, N. Avksent'ev, M. Vishnyak, A. Gukovsky and V. Rudnev. This essential journal is available on microfiche.


Days (Dni)
A newspaper which appeared first in Berlin and subsequently in Paris. It is of greater political than cultural import, although literary criticism by Khodasevich did appear there.


Essays (Opyty)
Literary almanacs published between 1953 and 1956 by Roman Grynberg et al in New York. This journal was the predecessor of Aerial Ways. Note: Through a mistake the English translation of this journal's title was listed as Experiments (the commonest dictionary translation for Opyty into English) rather than the intended Essays, and subsequently the listing had to be maintained on the title page for copyright reasons. The error is now corrected. This information was supplied to the bibliographer by Vladimir Nabokov.


Facets (Grani)
Literary anthologies edited by Sasha Chyorny and published in Berlin in 1923–24. Only two numbers appeared. Note: This Facets is not to be confused with the Munich-based journal of the same name in which Nabokov's verse

has been reprinted once but to which he has never contributed.

## Fire-Bird, The (Zhar-Ptitsa)

An elegant literary and artistic journal published in Berlin between 1921 and 1926.

## For Freedom (Za Svobodu)

An émigré daily newspaper published in Warsaw in the 1920s and early 1930s. It is of little cultural importance.

## Illustrated Russia (Illustrirovannaya Rossiya)

This journal, published in the 1920's, was, as its title indicates, a kind of Russian émirgé Life Magazine, but for that very reason it is valuable as virtually the only pictorial record of the emigration. Usually thought of as a Parisian publication, this journal was edited in Paris but published in Berlin.

## Latest News, The (Poslednie Novosti)

The most prominent émigré newspaper in the 1930s. It was edited by Pavel Miliukov and published in Paris between 1931 and 1939. There is a positive microfilm of this newspaper at Harvard University and limited years may also be found at the Bibliothèque Nationale in Paris.

## Link, The (Zveno)

An important émigré publication, first a weekly newspaper and then a journal, which was connected with The Latest News. Its editors were Pavel Miliukov and Maksim Vinaver, and it appeared between 1923 and 1928.

## Messenger of Europe, The (Vestnik Evropy)

One of the most prominent of the Russian pre-revolutionary "thick journals," The Messenger of Europe is available in many large universities and national libraries outside of Russia.

New Gazette, The (Novaya Gazeta)
A short-lived literary newspaper edited by Marc Slonim published in Paris in 1931. Only five numbers appeared.

New Review, The (Novyj Zhurnal)
The main surviving literary organ of the Russian emigration, The New Review was founded by M. Tsetlin and the well-known novelist Mark Aldanov in 1942. The quarterly succeeded Contemporary Annals and is still being published in New York. The present editor of The New Review is Roman Gul'.

New Russian Word, The (Novoe Russkoe Slovo)
The oldest émigré newspaper, The New Russian Word began to be published prior to 1917 and is still published daily in New York. There is a good chance that there exist some forgotten letters-to-the-editor by Nabokov in this paper during the 1940s.

New Word, The (Novoe Slovo)
One of the last Russian newspapers to appear in Berlin before World War II.

Northern Lights (Spolokhi)
This interesting Berlin literary journal was published between 1921 and 1923 by the poet A. Drozdov who subsequently returned to the Soviet Union.

Numbers (Chisla)
A journal of art and literature which was published in Paris between 1930 and 1934. Ten numbers appeared.

Our Age (Nash Vek)
A Berlin weekly newspaper published between 1930 and 1933(?). One of its editors was Iosif Hessen, and the newspaper continued the positions of The Rudder.

Our World (Nash Mir)

A short-lived Sunday supplement to The Rudder.

Renaissance (Vozrozhdenie)

An important émigré newspaper which appeared in Paris between 1925 and 1940. In recent years the title of this paper has been continued as a journal. Renaissance started as a daily newspaper in June, 1925. In 1936 it became a weekly paper, which ceased publication in June, 1940. The publication resumed as a journal in January, 1949, and is still appearing.

Rudder, The (Rul').

The leading Berlin émigré newspaper of the 1920s, and one of the most important sources for the early publications of Nabokov. The paper, of which Nabokov's father was a founder, appeared between 1920 and 1931. A very good though incomplete microfilm holding of the paper is at Harvard University.

Russia and Slavdom (Rossiya i Slavyanstvo)

A weekly newspaper, originally simply Russia (Rossiya), published between 1927 and 1931 by Pyotr Struve in Paris.

Russian Annals (Russkie Zapiski)

A quarterly periodical, similar in some respects to Contemporary Annals, which briefly attempted to unite Western European and Far Eastern émigré writing. It appeared between 1937 and 1939, was published first in Shanghai and Paris but later only in Paris, and was edited by Pavel Miliukov.

Russian Echo (Russkoe Èkho)

A weekly illustrated journal edited by B. Orechkin, first in Prague and then in Berlin, between 1922 and 1926(?).

Today (Segodnya)

A daily newspaper published in Riga, Latvia in the 1920s.

Virgin Soil (Nov')

A short series of magazine almanacs of high literary interest which began to appear in Tallin, Estonia in 1928.

Will of Russia, The (Volya Rossii)

The main journal of the emigration in Prague, The Will of Russia began as a weekly newspaper in 1922, then became a fortnightly, and between 1925 and 1932 was a monthly of the "thick journal" format, the only one in the emigration to maintain anything close to such regularity.

Word, The (Slovo)

One of the important émigré newspapers in the Baltic region, published in Riga in the early 1920s.

1. Interview with Claude Jannoud in Le Figaro Littéraire. Paris. January 13, 1973.
2. Forthcoming short story collection to be entitled Tyrants Destroyed and to include the following short stories: Tyrants Destroyed, A Nursery Tale, Music, Lik, Recruiting, Terror, The Admiralty Spire, A Matter of Chance, In Memory of L. I. Shigaev, Bachmann, Perfection, Vasily Shishkov, and The Vane Sisters. 1974
3. A collection of new and old reviews and essays, Strong Opinions. McGraw-Hill, New York
4. "Culture in Exile" ("Kultura v izgnanii") by Nikolay Andreyev in The Russian Standard (Znamya Rossii). Prague. 1936–37?
   The journal in which this article appeared was an annual cultural number published by a Prague religious association, Krest'yanskaya Russia.
5. Review of Invitation to a Beheading by B in The Facet (Gran'). No. 1. Paris. 1939
6. Review of The Real Life of Sebastian Knight by Mariya Tolstaya in The New Review (Novy Zhurnal). No. 2. New York. 1942
7. "The Art of Sirin" ("Tvorchestvo Sirina") by Marc Slonim in The New Russian Word (Novoe Russkoe Slovo). New York. September ?, 1944
8. Review of The Real Life of Sebastian Knight. Anonymous. In Bridges (Mosty). No. 5. Munich. 1960
9. Review of Pnin by Yakov Gorbov in Renaissance (Vozrozhdenie). No. 134. Paris. 1963

"About V. Sirin"—review  *1512*

*"About you I daydreamed so long ago, so often"*  *0255*

*Acropolis, The*  *0435*

**Ada**  *0887, 0889*

**Ada eller Ardor**  *0886*

Adamovich, Georgy—reviews by  *1427, 1432, 1436, 1448, 1455, 1460, 1467, 1489, 1492, 1493, 1496, 1501, 1529*

**Ada o dell'Ardore**  *0888*

**Ada; of Adoratie, een familie kroniek**  *0890*

**ADA OR ARDOR: A FAMILY CHRONICLE**  *0885*

*Admiraltejskaya igla*  *0838, 0957*

*Admiralty Needle, The*  *0838, 0957*

*"Admiring the tumultuous clouds"*  *0078*

*Aerial Island*  *0566*

*Aëroplan—"Kak poyot on, kak nezhdanno"*  *0286, 0536*

*Aëroplan—"Skol'znuv po stoptannoj trave"*  *0173*

*Affair of Honor, An*  *0881, 0898, 0934*

*After the Storm*  *0099, 0409*

**Agaspher**  *1065*

**L'Aguet**  *0698*

Aikhenval'd, Yu.—reviews by  *1401, 1402, 1408, 1414, 1419, 1421*

*Airplane, The—"How it sings, how unexpected"*  *0286, 0536*

*Airplane, The—"It slid along the trampled grass"*  *0173*

*"Akkordy, kak volny i prizrak razluki"*  *0063*

*Akropol'*  *0435*

**Albatross, The**  *1279*

Aldanov, M.—review of  *1150*

*Aleksandr Saltykov: Odes and Hymns*  *1110*

**Alice in Wonderland**—translation of  *1278*

*All-Forgiving, The*  *0157*

*"All I recall is piny fragrance"*  *0270*

*"All that constrains the heart"*  *0637*

*"All the windows you opened, the curtains you drew"*  *0261*

*"almonds at the crossroads blossom, The"*  *0093*

*Al principe S. M. Kacurin*  *0622*

*Alter Ego, "When Life is Torture . . ."*—translation of  *1295*

Amfiteatrov, Aleksandr—review by  *1426*

**Andere Ufer**  *1100*

*"And I beheld: the vaults of heavens darkened"*  *0105*

Andreev, Vadim—review by  *1480*

Andreyev, Nikolay—review by  *1465*

*"And the funereal . . ."*  *0506*

*"And those who've come from Earth to Paradise"*  *0481*

*Autumn—"The distance was that day deeper and lighter"*
  *0081*
*Autumn—"The leaves are falling. Disembodied chimes"*
  *0209, 0432*
*Avtomobil' v gorakh—Sonet   0490*
*Awakening, The   0578*
*Babochka   0212*
*Bakhman   0686, 0914*
Balakshin, Pyotr—review by   *1498*
*Ballad of Longwood Glen, The   0351, 0367, 0638, 1274*
*ballata della valletta di Longwood, La   0639*
*Bars   0472*
*Bashmachyok   0117*
Basilissa, a Tale of the Empress Theodora—review of   *1157*
**Bastaards** *0782*
*Bastardzeichen, Das   0780*
Bateau ivre, Le—translation of   *1284*
Beatrice—review of   *1140*
*Beauty, The   0754, 0965*
*"Beauty! Beauty! In it are mysteriously blended"   0051*
*"Bednoe serdtse do blednogo dnya"   0032*
*Bee, The   0130*
*Beetle, The   0460*
*Beginnings   0183*
*Belle Dame Sans Merci, La   0233*
*Belloc Essays—Mild But Pleasant   1164*
Belloc, Hilaire—review of   *1164*
*Belyj raj   0229, 0446*
**Benachrichtigung, Die** *0757*
**BEND SINISTER** *0779, 1256*
Berberova, N.—review by   *1537*
Berberova, N.—review of   *1146*
*Berlinskaya vesna   0517*
*Berlin Spring   0517*
*Beryoza v Vorontsovskom parke   0097*
*Beryozy   0222, 0419*
*"Be silent, don't stir up your soul"   0267, 0455*
Beskid, N.—review of   *1127*
*"Be with me more limpid and more simple"   0150*
*"Beyond the forest with a parting smile"   0009*
*Bezhentsy   0422*
*"Bez nadezhd ya zhdal"   0028*
*Bezumets   0389, 0583*
*"Bezvozvratnaya, vechno-rodnaya"   0191*

*"Big lindens, reeling, sang"*  0024
*Bil den' kak den'*  0403
*Bilet*  0544
*Biology*  0224
*Birches*  0222, 0419
*Birch Tree in the Vorontsov Park*  0097
Bitsilli, Pyotr—reviews by  1515, 1521
Bitter stuff—poems, review of  1114
Black and Azure—review of  1142
*Blades of Grass*  0161
*Blagost'*  0691, 0908
*"Blazhenstvo moyo, oblaka i blestyashchie vody"*  0219
*Blazon, The*  0374, 0511, 0512
Blessed Be Your Name—poems, review of  1128
*"blind man is playing his violin at the corner, A"*  0438
*Blizzard, The*  0145, 0409
Blokh, Andrei—review of  1119
Blokh, Raisa—review of  1122
*Bogi*  0917
*Bol'shaya Medveditsa*  0108
*"Bol'shie lipy, shatayas', peli"*  0024
*Bonfire, The*  0482
*Bonne Lorraine, La*  0291, 0373, 0501, 0502
*Bonne Lorraine, La*—review of  1401
"Books and People"—review of  1500, 1508, 1517
*Boxer's Girl, The*  0491
Bozhnev, B.—review of  1123
*Breaking the News*  0756, 0895, 0967, 0968
"Bremya pamyati—O Sirine"—review  1497
*Bricks*  0282, 0556
*Britva*  0925
Brodsky, Boris—review by  1416
Brooke, Rupert—translation of  1288
*"Bud' so mnoj prozrachnee i proshche"*  0150
Bulkin, A.—review of  1111
Bunin, Ivan—review of  1134
"Buninsky mir i Sirinsky mir"—review  1430
"Burden of Memory, The—On Sirin"—review  1497
*Busy Man, The*  0750, 0944
*Butterflies*  1080
Butterflies, Moths and Other Studies—review of  1212
*Butterfly, The*  0212
*Butterfly Collecting in Wyoming*  1215
*"Byl' den' kak den'. Dremala pamyat'. Dlilis'"*  0333

Enchanted Nightingale, The—review of  *1109*
*Enchanted Nightingale, a tale by Richard Dehmal, The*  1109
*Enchanting Season, An*  *0284, 0538*
**engano, El**  *0732*
*"Enough, farewell! I do not need an answer"*  *0064*
*Ensirakkaus*  *1047*
*Escenas de la vida de un monstruo doble*  *1053*
*Eshchyo bezmolvstvuyu*  *0370*
*"Eshchyo bezmolvstvuyu i krepnu ya v tishi"*  *0135*
*Esilio*  *1094*
*"Esli, byvalo, provodish' ves' den'"*  *0067*
*"Esli veter sud'ba, radi shutki"*  *0225, 0443*
*"Esli v'yotsya moj stikhi i letit i trepeshchet"*  *0115*
Essay on Nature, An—review of  *1158*
*"Est' son. On povtoryaetsya, kak tomnyj"*  *0637*
*"Est' v odinochestve svodoba"*  *0244*
*"Eternally young are my sorrows"*  *0010*
*"Ètot vecher luchistyj grustil nad lyud'mi"*  *0048*
*'Että Kerran Aleppossa'*  *1023*
*"Ètu zhizn' ya lyublyu isstuplyonnoj lyubov'yu"*  *0133*
**Eugene Onegin**—translation of  *1188, 1259, 1299*
*Evening of Russian Poetry, An*  *0340, 0358, 0614, 1268*
*"Evening is hazy and long, The"*  *0637*
*Evening on a Vacant Lot*  *0310, 0388, 0580*
**Event, The**  *1070*
**Event, The**—reviews of  *1519, 1920*
*Event from Life, An*  *0755, 0978*
*"Everlasting terror. The black quagmires."*  *0084*
*Execution, The*  *0289, 0380, 0549, 0550*
*Exhibition of M. Nakhman-Achariya, An*  *1129*
*Exile*  *0599*
*Exile (Izgnan'e)*  *0518*
*Exile*  *1093*
*Exiles, The*  *0422*
*Exodus*  *0503*
**EXPLOIT, THE**  *0725*
*Express, The*  *0277*
*L'extermination des tyrans*  *0996*
**EYE, THE**—novel  *0694, 0695, 0743*
**Eye, The**—novel, reviews of  *1462, 1466, 1468, 1469, 1496,*
   *1518, 1521*
**Eye, The**—short story collection  *0743*
*Eye, The*—short story  *0744*
*Eyes*  *0264*

*Grand Piano, The*   *0530*
*"Grasshopper sonorously echoes grasshopper"*   *0030*
*Grauen, Das*   *0930*
*Great Bear, The*   *0108*
*Griby*   *0457*
Grigorovich, V. S.—review of   *1118*
*Groza*—poem   *0473*
*Groza*—short story   *0685, 0915*
*"Groza rastayala. Nebo yasno"*   *0079*
**GROZD'**   *0241*
*Guardian Angel*   *0185*
Guerney, B. G.—review of   *1171*
*Guest, The*   *0290, 0495*
**Guetteur, Le**   *0699*
*Guidebook to Berlin*   *0687, 0923*
Guillotine at Work, The—review   *1167*
Gul', Roman—review   *1397*
Gusev, D.—review of   *1120*
**Habla, memoria!**   *1103*
Ham—poems, review of   *1121*
Hamlet—translation of   *1285, 1286*
**Han som spelade schack med livet**   *0677*
*Happiness*   *0006*
Harbage, Alfred—review of   *1166*
*Hazel and Birch*   *0098*
*Heart, The*   *0471*
**Heer, Vrouw, Boer**   *0663, 0664*
*"Here, in this dacha garden, we were happy"*   *0096*
**Hero of Our Time, A**—translation of   *1301*
Hero of Our Time, A—introduction to   *1184, 1257*
*"Her soul, like an extraordinary light"*   *0258*
**Het Oog**   *0702*
*"He was triangular, two-winged and legless"*   *0582*
*Hexameters*   *0471*
*"Historical Anecdotes [from old Calendars]"*   *1390*
*Home*   *0412*
*Homes for Dukhobors*   *1160*
*Homewards*   *0221*
*"Hommage à Franz Hellens"*   *1197*
*Horses*   *0230*
*Hotel Room*   *0371*
*"How alluring my North is in Spring"*   *0410*
*"How avidly holding one's breath"*   *0477*
*"However dismally and densely"*   *0265, 0455*

*"Khochetsya tak mnogo, khochetsya tak malo"* 0054
Khodasevich, Vladislav—reviews by *1429, 1439, 1451, 1461,*
   *1487, 1508, 1517, 1519, 1528*
Khodasevich, Vladislav—review of *1121*
Khodasevich, Vladislav—translation of *1296, 1296A*
Khokhlov, German—review by *1441, 1486*
*Khram* 0437
*Khudozhnik* 0162
*Khudozhnik-nishchij* 0226
*Khvat* 0749, 0972
*Kimono, A* 0169
*Kinematograf* 0551
*Kingdoms* 0180
**KING, QUEEN, KNAVE** 0656, 0657
**King, Queen, Knave**—reviews of *1420–1426, 1437, 1471*
*Kiparisy* 0134
*Kirpichi* 0282, 0556
Kiskevich, E.—review of *1118*
*K. kn. S. M. Kachurinu* 0332, 0402
Klots, A.—review of *1211*
*K muze* 0383, 0567
K-n., E.—review by *1399*
Knight in the Tiger's Skin, The—review of *1156*
*Knight's Betrothed, The* 0459
"Knigi i lyudi"—reviews *1500, 1508, 1517*
*Kn. S. M. Kachurinu* 0620
Knut, D.—review of *1123*
Kobyakov, D.—review of *1114*
*"Kogda moya ruka vo t'me tvoyu vstrechaet"* 0053
"Kogda na sklone let"—translation of *1276*
*"Kogda, s nebes na ètot bereg dikij"* 0090
*"Kogda, tumannye, my svidelis' vpervye"* 0254
*"Kogda ya po lesnitse almaznoj"* 0470
*"Kogda zakhochesh', ya ujdu"* 0259
*Komnata* 0300, 0535
Kondratovich, I.—review of *1118*
**Konge, Dame, Knaegt** *0664A*
*Koni* 0230
**König, Dame, Bube** *0662*
*Kon'kobezhets* 0510
*Kontrasty* 0058
Korev, S.—review by *1404*
**KOROL', DAMA, VALET** *0656*
*Korolyok* 0830, 0959

*Literaturnye zametki—O Vostavshikh Angelakh* 1141
"Literaturnye zametki"—reviews 1402, 1414, 1419
Literaturnyj Smotr—review of 1159
*"little marchioness knows, The"* 0154
*Little Shoe, The* 0117
*"Live. Do not murmur, do not number"* 0088
*Lodgings in Trinity Lane* 1092
**Lolita**—screenplay 1076
**LOLITA** 0793–0795, 0797–0800, 0802–0805, 0807–0810,
  0812–0816, 0818, 0819, 0821, 0822, 0824–0826
**Lolita**—review of 1536
"Lolita" 0643
*"Lolita" and Mr. Girodias* 1194
**Lo li t-ai** 0801
"Lolita and the Splitting of the Atom"—review 1535
"Lolita i Raspad Atoma"—review 1535
*"Lost forever, forever my own"* 0191
*Lunar Lines* 0644
*Lunar Reverie* 0042, 0407
*Lunnaya gryoza* 0042, 0407
*Lunnaya noch'* 0107
*Lunnyj svet* 0043
Lur'e, V.—review by 1398
**Lushins Verteidigung** 0672
Luther, Arthur—review by 1470
*Luzinin Puolustus* 0669
L'vov, Lollij—reviews by 1459, 1491
*Lysandra cormion, a New European Butterfly* 1201
*"Lyublyu v struyashchejsya dremote"* 0195
*Lyublyu ya goru* 0376
*"Lyudyam ty skazhesh': nastalo"* 0238
*Lyzhnyj pryzhok* 0529
M, Ars.—review by 1410
**Ma'dabat Al-dhi'āb** 0767
*Mademoiselle O* 0787, 0870, 1008–1012, 1077
*Madman, The* 0389, 0583, 0584
**Magda** 0716
"Magic and Madness in Chess"—review 1484
*Magician, The* 1061
**Maguda** 0716
*Mailbox, The* 0283
Majer, Nikita—review by 1532
**Man from the USSR, The** 1067
**Man from the USSR, The**—reviews of 1416

*Room, The   0300, 0535, 0623*
*Room, The   0341, 0359*
**Rorita**   *0811*
Rosimov, G.—review by   *1396*
*Rossiya   0458*
*Rossiya—"Ne vsyo-li ravno mne—raboj-li, nayomnitsej"*
    *0132, 0421*
Rostaveli, Shotha—review of   *1156*
Rothenstein, J. K.—review of   *1161*
Rowe, William—review of   *1196*
*Rowe's Symbols   1196*
*Royal'   0530*
*Rozhdestvenskie stikhi   0509*
*Rozhdestvenskij rasskaz   0932*
*Rozhdestvo—poem   0271*
*Rozhdestvo—short story   0684, 0918*
*Rupert Brooke   1108*
*Rus   0239*
*Rusalka   0140, 0600, 1075*
*Russia   0458*
**RUSSIAN BEAUTY, A**—short story collection   *0891*
*Russian Beauty, A—short story   0892*
"Russian Literature in Emigration"—reviews   *1447, 1451,*
    *1452*
*Russian River, The   0500*
*Russia—"What do I care if a slavegirl or hireling"   0132,*
    *0421*
"Russkaya literatura v èmigratsii"—reviews   *1447, 1451,*
    *1452*
*Russkaya reka   0500*
"Russkie Novinki"   *1433*
*"S dozhdyom i vetrom boryatsya beryozy"   0080*
*"S serogo severa"   0406, 0646*
*Saint Petersburg—"Come, Leila, misty one, to me!"   0492*
Saltykov, Aleksandr—review of   *1110*
*"Sam treugol'nyj, dvukrylyj, beznogij"   0582*
*Sankt Peterburg—"Ko mne, tumannaya Leila!"   0492*
Saranna, Zinaida—review   *1490*
Sartre, J. P.—review of   *1179*
Savel'ev, A.—reviews by   *1407, 1431, 1433, 1438, 1450, 1456,*
    *1463, 1475, 1485*
Savel'ev, R. S.—review by   *1518*
Sazanov, Yu.—review by   *1478*
*Scenes from the Life of a Double Monster   0869, 1052, 1252*

Sidorov, D.—review of *1118*
**Sie kommt-kommt sie?** *0653*
*Signalen en symbolen* *1043*
Signs and Symbols *0862, 1039, 1250*
Silence of the Sea, The—review of *1164*
**Silma** *0697*
*Sily* *0181*
*"simple song, a simple sadness, A"* *0144, 0439*
*Siren'* *0293, 0558*
"Sirin as a 'Soulless' Writer or P. Balakshin as a Thoughtless
    Critic"—review *1499*
"Sirin 'Bezdushnyj' Pisatel' ili P. Balakshin Bezdumnyj
    Kritik"—review *1499*
"Sirin"—reviews *1465, 1492, 1505*
"Sirin's *The Event* in the Russian Theatre"—review *1519*
*Skater, The* *0510*
*Skazanie iz apokrifa* *0434*
*Skazaniya* *0415*
*Skazka* *0683, 0926*
*Skif* *0127*
*Skijump, The* *0529*
*Skital'tsy*—poem *0484*
**Skital'tsy**—play *1066*
**Skratt i mörkret** *0723*
*"sky sweeps along, palpitating and blazing, The"* *0146*
*Slava* *0327, 0398, 0601*
Slava Bohu, The Story of the Dukhobors—review of *1160*
*Sličný* *1000*
Slonim, Marc—review by *1445*
*"Slonyayus' pereulkami bez tseli"* *0477*
*Sluchaj iz zhizni* *0755, 0978*
*Sluchajnost'* *0912*
**Smert'** *1063*
*Smert' Pushkina* *0493*
*Smert'—"Utikhnet zhizni rokot zhadnyj"* *0494*
*Smert'—"Vyjdut angely navstrechu"* *0155*
*"Smeyotsya kraska, smeyotsya liniya"* *0011*
*Snapshot, The* *0285, 0378, 0545, 0546*
*Sneg* *0385, 0569*
Snesareva-Kazakova, N.—review of *1128*
*Snezhnaya noch'* *0459*
*Snimok* *0285, 0378, 0545*
*Snovidenie* *0295, 0377, 0541*
*Snow* *0385, 0569, 0570*

Struve, Gleb—reviews by *1403, 1417, 1420, 1423, 1440, 1444, 1449, 1483, 1512, 1514, 1516, 1533A*
"Suffocating World, A"—review *1511*
*Suflyor 0450*
*Sui governanti 0618*
*Summer Day, A 0069*
*Summer Night 0013*
*Summit, The 0524*
*Sun, The 0298*
*Sun of the Sleepless 0106*
*Sunset, At 0392*
Supervielle—translation of *1289*
*Svyatki 0288, 0480*
*Swallow, The*—translation of *1295*
*Swallows 0198*
*"Syad' poblizhe ko mne. My pripomnim s toboj" 0061*
*Systarna Vane 1060*
*Szenen aus dem Leben eines Doppelungeheurers 1054*
*Taferelen uit het leven van een tweevondig monster 1055*
*Tajnaya Vecherya 0199, 0418*
*"Takogo net moshennika vtorogo" 1394*
*Tamara 1088*
Tauber, E.—review by *1530*
Tauber, E.—review of *1118*
*"Tebya, tebya odnu, lyubit' ya obeshchayu" 0018*
*Telegrafnye stolby 0193*
*Telegraph Poles 0193*
*Temporale, Il 0916*
*Ten' 0297, 0523*
Tennyson—translation of *1281*
Terapiano, Yu.—review by *1506*
*Terra incognita 0747, 0899, 0945–0948, 1244*
*Terror 0693, 0929, 1414*
*Terror*—reviews of *1413, 1415*
*"Terzaem ya utrachennymi dnyami" 0498*
Thaler, Alwin—review of *1166*
Thanksgiving—translation of *1300*
*'That in Aleppo Once. . . .' 0790, 0867, 1022, 1248*
*"That night I could but sob with rapture" 0046*
*"There are such moments: 'it can't be', you mutter" 0640*
*"There is one path and a great many roads" 0498*
*"There is this dream, repeating like the languid" 0637*
*"There's liberty in solitude" 0244*